MUTHULAI

*A Trailblazer in Surgery and
Women's Rights*

VR DEVIKA

PAPER
MISSILE

NIYOGI
BOOKS

Published by
NIYOGI BOOKS
Block D, Building No. 77,
Okhla Industrial Area, Phase-I,
New Delhi-110 020, INDIA
Tel: 91-11-26816301, 26818960
Email: niyogibooks@gmail.com
Website: www.niyogibooksindia.com

Text © VR Devika

Editor: Shalini Arun
Layout: Shashi Bhushan Prasad
Cover design: Anurag Hira
Cover illustrator: Douluri Narayana

ISBN: 978-93-91125-67-7
Publication: 2022

Publisher's note: Every effort has been made to ensure the accuracy of the
information presented in this book. The images used in this book come from
either the public domain or from the public commons, unless otherwise
stated. The publisher welcomes comments and feedback from readers, in
order to improve future editions, at niyogibooks@gmail.com.

Printed at Niyogi Offset Pvt. Ltd., New Delhi, India

To

Keshav Desiraju,
who himself had wanted to write a biography
of Dr Muthulakshmi Reddy,
and read the manuscript meticulously in
the hours before his last breath;
to
Dr V. Shanta,
who wanted this book written;
and
to the marvellous women of
Avvai Home and WIA who were the motivation.

'Muthulakshmi Reddy was a reformer from the inside, as it were like Dr Ambedkar was. Which is different from being like a corrector from the outside. That was her strength. But I do wish she had a vein of art in her as well, that could have enabled her to see and say that the tradition she wanted to abolish had a precious possession within it that needed salvaging, protecting and nurturing. We cannot, of course, have everything that we want our way. Muthulakshmi plus art, Balasarasvati minus seclusion, Rukmini Devi plus Sringara, Subbulakshmi minus Sanskritisation. These are our wish-lists, based on our predispositions and prejudices. Each of these icons had guiding passions and pursued them, fufilling their individual destinies. We cannot shape to suit our ideals. We are not their *bhagyavidhata*s!

—Gopalkrishna Gandhi

CONTENTS

AUTHOR'S NOTE

Reddy or Reddi? Even Muthulakshmi seemed to be confused. She and her son have used the two spellings frequently. Reddy or Reddi, Muthulakshmi was ready for long battles at different periods of her life to achieve some seemingly impossible tasks. A Google doodle that appeared on 30 July 2019, marking Dr Muthulakshmi Reddy's 133rd birth anniversary, (she was born on 30 July 1886), shows her as a pioneer pathcreator for women.

I began to study Dr Muthulakshmi Reddy seriously in 1985 when Geeta Dharmarajan and I started a project at Avvai Home. Later, Avvai Home requested my help for a production on Dr Reddy; I read her autobiography, papers, interviewed her son Dr Krishnamurthy, her disciple Dr.V. Shanta and her associate Sarojini Varadappan for the production which was directed by Pralayan of Chennai Kalai Kuzhu. I realised her story needed to be told, since her written work was being used to denigrate her, her actions needed to be showcased. Talking to women who benefitted from her activism revealed a thinking that the highly educated had ambiguous ideas about the ideologies of pioneers. The poorest of poor wondered about the difficulties they must have faced when they carved a new path, when they could have easily lived in their privileged circumstances.

I decided to take every opportunity possible to give a talk about and write articles on her. Every talk became a new learning. I was urged by Dr V. Shanta to write a new biography of Dr Reddy.

I wish to thank the people who encouraged and helped me in this task. My dear friend Hema Ramanathan who looked at the first copy and encouraged with useful comments; Prof. S. Swaminathan who shared many stories about Pudukkottai with me; Nesa Arumugham who was kind and encouraging as she always is; S. Anandhi of MIDS who had the patience to go through this non-academic work and appreciate it; Gitanjali Kolanad with her unconventional thinking, gave valuable comments. Narmadha's PhD thesis on the Tamil Devadasi tradition and B. Jeevasundari's biography of Muvalur Ramamirthammal helped in a better understanding of the issue. V. Sushila, sister of Dr V. Shanta, created a space for me at her office in Avvai Home to browse through records and papers, and also gave access to pictures. Wonderful conversations with the relatives of Dr Muthulakshmi Reddy, particularly P. Krishnamurthi, her grandnephew on the paternal side, and Swami Dayanand, her grandnephew on the maternal side, helped to put things into perspective. Her grandchildren Dr Lakshmi Bhattacharyya and Dr Krishnamurthi Sundaram spoke at length about their grandmother. Grandnieces Dr Uma and her sisters, and Ram Suryanarayan, a grandnephew, were full of enthusiasm to talk. So were Janaki, who grew up in Avvai Home, Punita, who studied there, and dancer and historian Jeetendra Hirschfeld. I am indebted to all these people who have made this biography possible.

Special thanks to Gopalkrishna Gandhi who sent a quote on her, Shalini Arun who edited this book, to Nirmal Kanti Bhattacharjee and Niyogi Books for agreeing to publish it, Trisha Niyogi for her warm conversations and to Mini Krishnan for introducing me to them.

This is a labour of love.
V.R. Devika

BREAKING STEREOTYPES

'A girl has got 100 per cent in surgery!...An Indian girl!'

Lt. Col. William James Niblock jumped up from his seat and ran down the corridor of the Red building of the Madras Medical College with a sheet of paper in his hand, screaming....

A boy scoring cent per cent would have generated enough excitement in the college, but a girl? And an Indian girl at that? A girl from a small town, who had been home schooled? In 1912?[1]

C.N. Muthulakshmi Ammal was amused even as her classmates clapped around her. She remembered how Lt. Col. Niblock had tried to dissuade her, five years earlier, from seeking admission to the MB and CM (Bachelor of Medicine and Master of Surgery) degree, advising her to take the easier L.M. and S. (Degree of Licentiate in Medicine and Surgery) course instead. Her father S. Narayanasami Iyer and she had travelled all the way from Pudukkottai, 380 kilometres away in the south to Madras, now Chennai, in the British Presidency. The year was 1907 and there were few Indian girls in the formal education system provided by the British rulers.

Lt. Col. Niblock had thought the girl was too frail and timid to be able to manage the tough MB & CM course. He felt that as a woman, she may have too delicate a heart to withstand long hours in surgery and might faint at the sight of blood. Muthulakshmi had smiled to herself thinking that with menstruation and giving birth, girls see enough blood in their lives.[2] She insisted on joining the course.

Narayanasami also had to use his persuasive powers, and his confidence in his daughter's intelligence and studiousness, to secure admission to the course. He had even suggested that the girl may be transferred to the licentiate degree if she failed to get good grades in the first year of the MB and CM course.[3]

Here she was at the end of the course—topping her class. Winning most medals and prizes for competency that year! At the convocation, as Muthulakshmi went up to the dais to receive the gold medals, she glanced at her father in the audience, beaming with happiness. She thought of the sacrifices he had made to bring her there.

She also expressed silent gratitude to Raja Bhairava Martanda Tondaiman, the king of the princely state of Pudukkottai, who, brushing aside all objections, had encouraged and supported her studies monetarily.

Narayanasami Iyer was the principal of H.H. Raja's college and a tutor to the Pudukkottai royal family. He spent his time between the palace and the college, and was well regarded in Pudukkottai. He dressed well and walked tall. The king of Pudukkottai would, on the way back from the army parade ground after his morning exercises, get down from his car to pay his respects if he saw Narayanasami sitting majestically on the *tinnai* (pyol) Narayanasami also enjoyed being acknowledged in the streets by his students, many of whom were from prominent families of Pudukkottai. Fond of music and dance, his spacious house on the Tanjore Main Street in Machuvadi hosted many artists of traditional Carnatic music and Bharathanatyam.[4] Muthulakshmi was privileged as the daughter of this educated and liberal Brahmin man who gave her the much-desired access to formal learning.

However, Muthulakshmi faced discrimination on account of being the daughter of Chandrammal, who belonged to the Melakkara community. The women of the community were trained in music and dance, and were permitted to perform in temple processions and rituals, and for the public on social occasions. Marriage in the conventional sense was barred for them according to religious rules, but they could be chosen by an upper caste male patron of means as a companion outside his own legal marriage. The children born in such relationships were not formally acknowledged by the fathers. Most members of the Melakkara community carried the name of the village or town they hailed from as identity, like Tirugokarnam Kanakambujam or Tiruvalaputtur Kalyani.

Narayanasami's Brahmin community and the Melakkara community lived around the temple in Tirugokarnam, just a street apart. Though there was much mingling between the two communities over music and performance, and a great respect for that knowledge that the Melakkara community held, there was always an understanding that the Brahmins were superior, and the unwritten rules were well known to all.[5] However, Muthulakshmi's case was different as Narayanasami acknowledged paternity of his children, contrary to the prevalent practice.[6] His enormous interest in their upbringing and education set him apart from other men of his stature in Pudukkottai. C.N. Muthulakshmi also carried both her parents' identifiers: C. for Coviloor, Chandrammal's native village, and N for Narayanasami Iyer, probably a first in those times.[7] But in her childhood, she was constantly made aware, with certain sights and comments by others around her, of belonging to her mother's community, a few notches lower in the social ladder of caste and class to her father's family.

It was King Raja Ramachandra Tondaiman's sister who had made a special request to Narayanasami, who was probably thirty, to be the patron at the *Bottukattudal* (being dedicated in a ritual marriage to a deity) of eleven-year-old Chandrammal, a beautiful and intelligent girl. Narayanasami's wife Sivakamu was a simple and naïve woman. Their two children had died in infancy. Narayanaswami lived in a joint family comprising his parents, elder brothers, their wives and children.[8] In order to maintain good relations with them, he complied with his family's demands of not partaking in any meal in Chandrammal's home, even carrying his own drinking water from home, as eating with non-Brahmins was prohibited. But his relationship with Chandrammal was very public and transparent.

Pudukkottai gradually, though reluctantly, came to accept this arrangement.

Chandrammal was barely sixteen when Muthulakshmi was born, on 30 July 1886. Of the eight infants she gave birth to, only four, three girls and a boy, survived: Muthulakshmi, Sundarambal, Ramiah and Nallamuthu. Chandrammal matched Narayanasami with her natural intelligence, charm and ever helpful nature. The people who interacted with her, even some members of Narayanasami's family loved her,[9] despite her strict and stubborn streak of calling a spade a spade.

Ramiah, as the only son, was of course given the special treatment by Chandrammal. Muthulakshmi who was fond of her brother remembered him as a mischievous boy, getting into trouble all the time but was always affectionately let off by his mother, who was stricter with the girls.

Ramiah fell ill with malaria, becoming weak and anaemic, and drastically lost weight. Chandrammal became hysterical and tried all kinds of medicines, and finally, on someone's advice brought home a Muslim healer. Muthulakshmi observed closely as the healer made a doll representing Ramiah with wet flour, pronounced some incantations and left. Muthulakshmi sat by the boy, conscientiously applying a wet cloth to his forehead to bring down the fever, till he recovered. Chandrammal was convinced it was the healer who had saved her son, and sent him generous gifts.[10]

At the age of four, Muthulakshmi was made to sit in the school on the *tinnai* (a platform fronting traditional houses for informal meetings) near her Machuvadi home. Narayanasami is said to have jokingly told the teacher that she should be taught enough Tamil to be able to keep milk and dhobi accounts. The elderly teacher sat on a raised mud platform and carved Tamil letters on palm leaves with a sharp pointed iron tool. Parents bought the palm leaves compiled as little books, generating a little income for the informal school. A young monitor, *Sattampillai* (noise caretaker), maintained discipline with a cane in his hand. He was kinder to girl students and hesitated to cane them.[11]

There was much criticism, and plenty of gossip, in Pudukkottai that Narayanasami was giving too much liberty to his daughters and his companion Chandrammal. But this did not deter him in his ever eager efforts to expand the horizon of his children through education.

Muthulakshmi endured unkind remarks from boys who would stand at road corners as she walked to the

Nellumandi Baliah School with a writing slate in hand. 'Here is a daughter of a Thevaradiyar (a corruption of the word 'devdasi', used in the Melakkara community for women dedicated to God in a ritual marriage but were partners to the male members with no strings attached) going to school,' they would shout. To avoid the boys, she chose to walk through smaller lanes and by-lanes. Once she reached the school, she felt safe and happy. She always stopped at the Vinayakar temple on the way, praying for good marks, and for a quiet journey to school and back home.[12]

Chandrammal's family had rejoiced at the birth of a girl child who could be dedicated to the temple and become the earning member in the family of musicians and dancers. But in Narayanasami's upper caste family, girls were seen as a burden, to be married off as early as possible. Chandrammal decided to get Muthulakshmi married to a relative when she turned ten. Fortunately for Muthulakshmi, a death in her mother's family the very week of the wedding precluded the ceremonies from taking place.

Narayanasami indulged his eldest daughter. He took her for long walks and told her tales about Pudukkottai. 'The Tondaiman dynasty', he told her, 'began in

Pudukkottai region when, in 1686, the Raja of Ramnad ousted a chief called Pallavarayan and appointed his brother-in-law Ragunatha Raya Tondaiman, the brother of his queen Kathayi Nachiar, as the new ruler.' In later centuries, the Tondaiman rulers, while nominally feudatories of the Ramnad state, often pursued an independent foreign policy. Raghunatha Tondaiman fought against the Nayaks of Tanjore in support of the Nayaks of Madurai and later fought with the Nayaks of Thanjavur and conquered Thirukkattupalli, a strategic place. The next ruler Raja Vijaya Reghunatha Raya Thondaiman was installed as Raja of Pudukkottai shortly after the death of his father and the self-immolation of his mother. He was 10 years old at the time. The Madras Government run by the East India Company asked Major William Blackburne, Resident of Tanjore, to undertake the management of the province of Pudukkottai and the guardianship of the minor king and his brother.

Muthulakshmi and her siblings knew that the name Pudukkottai was derived from the Tamil words *Pudu* which means 'new' and *Kottai* meaning 'fort'. They learnt that the place had an ancient history, having been mentioned in the ancient Sangam literature of Tamils (100 BCE to 250 BCE).

Narayanasami further expanded that the ancient Tamil work, *Silappadikkaram*, mentions Kodumbai or Kodumbalur in Pudukkottai which the protagonists Kovalan and Kannagi cross on their way to Madurai. The earliest Tamil epic mentions Kodumbai as lying on the highway between Uraiyur, the Chozha capital and Madurai, the Pandya capital.[13]

Narayanasami Iyer spoke proudly of the ancient temple in Kodumbalur, the architecture of which may have inspired the great Raja Rajeswaram or Brihadeeswara temple of Thanjavur, both of which do not have a foundation dug below the surface.[14] Muthulakshmi was impressed by the architectural skill of the times in constructing such incredibly heavy and tall structures with the technology of piling-on arrangement.[15] The splendour of Pudukkottai's heritage was the cradle on which the children of Chandrammal grew bright and curious, devouring whatever books their father brought home from his college library.

Being a naturally bright student, Muthulakshmi attracted the attention of Balakrishna Iyer aka Baliah, the headmaster of Nellumandi school, literally Paddy Market, (now called Sri Kulapathi Baliah Higher Secondary School in his honour). His was a magical presence in the school. A tall man at the sight of whom students would shiver, but also revere, as he represented a modern edition of the old priest cum teacher.[16]

When she attained puberty, questions arose about her further studies. Muthulakshmi insisted on studying further while her mother argued for marriage. Baliah pleaded with Chandrammal to let her continue her education.[17] He became extremely fond of Muthulakshmi and kept in regular touch with her family regarding her progress. Her father employed a private tutor on a payment of Rs 2 a month for one year, to teach Fourth Form subjects at home as there was no school for girls at those levels in Pudukkottai. Subsequently, he himself tutored her for a couple of hours a day to clear Fifth and Sixth Forms, laying a strong foundation for her higher education.

In 1902, a hundred students of Pudukkottai wrote the Matriculation examination. Only ten passed the exam with Muthulakshmi, the only girl, topping the list. This was quite a sensation in Pudukkottai, and her father was overjoyed. Though invited to teach at an elementary school, Muthulakshmi was keen to study further, even as her mother pestered her to get married. She wanted to go to St. Joseph's College in Trichy or the women's college in Palayamcottah but since these colleges had no women's hostel attached, there was no choice but to apply to the H.H. Raja's College for Men in Pudukkottai, though it was only second grade, and no girl had studied there.[18] Narayanasami appealed to the Raja for help in the admission process. Raja Bhairava Martanda Tondaiman, impressed with the letter of interest that Muthulakshmi wrote in English, decided to admit her.

People were aghast that such a thing was even being considered. In fact, the principal of the college wrote to the Darbar, the Raja's court. 'I do not think it is advisable to admit her into the regular class and train her along with the students, who are boys, as I believe that such a procedure will demoralise the boys.' The councillor and the Diwan supported the principal's view. The Diwan observed, 'The policy of having all along been not to allow girls of the Melagar caste into the Sirkar Girls High School in the town, and the furthering of the education of a girl of that caste not appearing to me to help the cause of female education in the state, I doubt it is advisable...'[19]

Parents threatened to pull their wards out of the college if a girl with such antecedents was made to sit with them in the class. A teacher threatened to resign. The Raja decided to give Muthulakshmi provisional admission telling her that her behaviour would be observed for three months, and if found good, other girls might get an opportunity too. Elaborate arrangements were made to help boys not get 'corrupted' by the presence of a girl. A screen was tied across the classroom, dividing it in two so that Muthulakshmi was visible only to the teacher and not to the boys. At the end of the day, a bell rang after she left the college building, and only then could the boys come out of their classrooms.

In college, Muthulakshmi enjoyed English and Sanskrit classes, taught by Professor B.V. Kameswara Iyer. He became fond of Muthulakshmi, and kept in touch with her long after her graduation, even looking her up in Madras during her medical studies. She was most interested in history taught by Ramachandra Sastrigal. 'He made his classes so interesting that students would eagerly await his classes,' Muthulakshmi wrote in her autobiography.[20] Acknowledging her remarkable success in the Intermediate programme, Radhakrishnan, the principal who had earlier objected to Muthulakshmi's admission, wrote to Narayanasami that he had never met a more intelligent and studious girl as Muthulakshmi. As the final barrier fell, her classmates honoured her with an intercaste dinner. A first again.

There was plenty of criticism from neighbours and relatives about Muthulakshmi's stubbornness in refusing marriage and her insistence on formal education. Chandrammal did not see any value in educating a girl in the formal system. She frequented temples and conducted pujas for her eldest daughter's marriage. and for grandchildren.

A distressed Muthulakshmi raised the idea with her father that it would be better for her to go away from Pudukkottai for further studies. As luck would have it, Dr Srinivasa Rao, an old student of Narayanasami Iyer, who happened to visit Pudukkottai suggested that Muthulakshmi could apply for a medical degree in Madras. That lifted her heart.[21]

During this time Chandrammal fell ill with typhoid, and Muthulakshmi looked after her diligently. When it seemed the end was near, in desperation, Muthulakshmi prayed fervently. Relatives and friends visited to say a final goodbye as she had been a popular person and well loved in the town.[22] Narayanasami sat by the bedside weeping, when someone mentioned that a doctor from the U.S. was visiting Pudukkottai hospitals. Dr Van Allen was requested to see her as a last-ditch effort. But by the time he arrived,

Chandrammal had gained consciousness and was able to follow his instruction during the examination. He prescribed a medicine and she soon recovered. This incident strengthened Muthulakshmi's resolve to get a medical degree.[23]

By then, as a result of a difference of opinion with the Diwan of Pudukkottai, Narayanasami had resigned his job as the principal of Raja's college, and as the director of public instruction of Pudukkottai.

Sir A. Sashiah Sastri, had become the Diwan of Pudukkottai in 1878. He worked on various social issues such as the improvement of temples, prevention of pox and strengthening of the education system. He instituted processes for safeguarding public health. He reorganised the budgetary practices and planned for town improvement. The police, courts, public works and a host of miscellaneous subjects of government received Sashiah Sastri's careful attention.[24] He was so popular that even years later, in the 1950s and 1960s, many houses in Pudukkottai had his framed picture on their walls.[25]

On the death of the Raja, his grandson, adopted formally to ensure succession, was installed as king in a *pattabhishekham* (coronation) ceremony on 2 May 1886, just two months before Muthulakshmi was born.

Sastri became Diwan Regent to the eleven-year-old Raja Martanda Bhairava Tondaiman.

At the legal age of nineteen, the young king assumed the full powers of the Raja of Pudukkottai in a formal durbar to which a large number of dignitaries and well-wishers were invited, including the Governor of the Madras Presidency, Lord Wenlock, and the family of Narayanasami.

Educated by a European tutor, the young king acquired a preference for the western mode of life.[26] He travelled widely, visiting Britain and Europe several times. In 1915, he went to Australia and married Esme Marie Fink, the daughter of a barrister. With prominent citizens of Pudukkottai beginning to take an active part in the Indian independence movement after the return of Mohandas Karamchand Gandhi from South Africa, Raja Martanda Bhairava Tondaiman decided to live outside India.

Narayanasami appealed to Raja Martanda Bhairava Tondaiman for help for Muthulakshmi's higher education in Madras. Pleased with the girl's enthusiasm and intelligence, the liberal Raja sanctioned a scholarship of Rs 50 a month and Rs 180 for books, for her to go to Madras to study for a medical degree.[27]

As Muthulakshmi prepared to leave for Madras, she walked around Pudukkottai and its surrounding areas where she had spent all her childhood, that echoed with connections to both her parents' heritages. Historically, Pudukkottai was a land of battles and battlements.[28] The Vellaru River flowing through Pudukkottai had served as a natural boundary for the famous Tamil kingdoms of Pallava, Chola, Pandya and later of the Vijayanagara empire. The rich farmlands immediately north of the river, Konadu or the King's country, and the wild undergrowth south of the river, Kanadu or the forest country,[29] were wealthy agricultural enterprises and enabled exploration of artistic pursuits.

History professor Ramachandra Sastrigal had, in his class, extolled the significance of the ancient rock-cut cave temples and edicts in the Nartamalai cluster of hills nearby. Muthulakshmi now took a fresh look at the megalithic burial sites within five kilometres of any point in Pudukkottai, which she had taken for granted while growing up. She also learnt of the darker history of Aluruttimalai or the 'man rolling hill', named for the practice of executing criminals by hurtling them down the hill.

Kudimiyanmalai (the hill of the God with the tuft of hair) has a temple for Shikhanatha where legend has it that the stone idol sprouted natural hair tied up in a tuft to support his devoted priest. The name Kudumiyamalai is explained in the Pudukkottai State Manual[30]. The legend goes that once the temple priest gave his lover the flowers intended for divine worship. When the ruler unexpectedly arrived in the temple, he offered him the flowers worn by his lover as *prasadam*. The king noticed few strands of hair in it and asked for an explanation. To conceal his offense, the priest asserted that the God himself had natural hair, all the time praying to the lord to save him. His prayers were heard and a *kudumi* or lock of hair miraculously appeared on the linga. The ceiling of the mandapa in front of the sanctum sanctorum of the deity Akhilandesvari (consort to Shikhanatha) was a reminder of Chandrammal's heritage. It is decorated with signs of the zodiac, and Muthulakshmi made the connection to ancient Tamil music in which the notes were represented in the zodiac. The famous musical inscription in Grantha script and Sanskrit language carved on the Southside of the rock cut shrine caught the attention of the scholarly Muthulakshmi.

Muthulakshmi and her siblings walked to the caves at Sittanavasal village, 15 km away to have a look at the beautiful paintings of dancing girls with their broad hips, slender waists and elaborate ornaments, recalling the beauty of the apsaras of mythology, their poses and expression suggesting rhythm and dynamic movement were examples of early Jain frescos. They also looked up the inscriptions which talk about repairs conducted at the time of Srimara Srivallabha Pandya, which can be dated to the 9th century. The caves then must have been excavated much earlier, thought Muthulakshmi.

The siblings visited the Viralimalai granite hill notable for the famed Shanmuganathar temple, and the innumerable peacocks enshrined as the vehicle of the god Muruga. Legend has it that in this renowned seat of Bharathanatyam, there were separate dancers for each of the thirty-two *adavus* or unit movements. On Mahasivarathri, the entire family would attend the *Viralimalai Kuravanji* dance drama performed as an all-night show to a large crowd. Muthulakshmi knew the troubles, travails, joys and ecstasies of the dancing community through the stories told by her maternal relatives.

At the great Brihadambal temple in Tirugokarnam, the daily evening worship would be followed by a music concert and a variety of dance performances like *kummi*, *kolattam*, *ammanai* and Bharathanatyam by girls.

Pudukkottai was also dotted with creative terracotta sculptures of the warrior deities known as Ayyanars. These large horse sculptures and the guardian deities, conspicuously located at the border of villages, are believed by villagers to protect them from evil spirits and the wrath of nature.

Muthulakshmi and her siblings also witnessed the famous Jallikkattu of Pudukkottai, celebrated as a quasi-religious indigenous sport conducted to propitiate the village deities.

All these sights and experiences seemed so special, now that she was leaving town.

As Muthulakshmi and her father boarded the boat mail on the main railway line to Madras Central, her siblings and mother Chandrammal looked on teary-eyed.

Muthulakshmi had seen her mother's community not being allowed beyond a point into the house of Brahmins, and if they drank water or the sweet payasam offered, it was in a different kind of cup from the ones the hosts drank in. They had to wash the vessel after use and keep it aside for further purification.[31] All these experiences had made the timid, frail girl extremely determined to make a difference in society with the education she was seeking.

Martanda Bhairava Tondaiman could not have known at that time that the simple and bright girl he was helping in her studies, was actually embarking on an extraordinary journey, and that her work would impact thousands of lives for several generations.

FOX HILL AND
THE RED BUILDING

Education, Freedom and Responsibility bring out the best
from the individual and race. This will apply to all men
and women irrespective of caste, creed or colour.

—Dr Muthulakshmi Reddy[1]

1907. The year Albert Einstein began to apply the laws of gravity to the theory of relativity; the year Maria Montessori opened her first school in Rome. It was also the year when Mohandas Karamchand Gandhi made his appearance in a South African court where he pleaded guilty, asking for a maximum punishment for leading the protest against the Transvaal Act, where every Indian was expected to register or be deported.

1907 was also the year when a young girl, alongwith her father, arrived in Madras; Muthulakshmi and her father Narayanasami went to the house of P.S. Krishnaswamy Iyer, an engineer with the Public Works Department and a former student of Narayanasami

Iyer in Pudukkottai. Krishnaswamy Iyer, his wife Dharmasamvardhini, also called Dharmambal and their sons Swaminathan, Venkataraman and Srinivasa Sanjivi greeted them warmly.

After some shopping in Mylapore, the father-daughter duo walked up to Luz Corner to catch the tram that came down from Santhome Church on the beach to Moore Market near the Central station, where they spent time buying books for Muthulakshmi's medical studies.[2] She was anxious and nervous but also full of aspiration. Her father carried a glowing letter of introduction from one of the brothers of the Raja of Pudukkottai.

All that young Muthulakshmi possessed at the time was confidence and a clear determination to study to become a doctor, at a time when it was rare for girls to complete even high school. She did not expect to have to push strongly to be admitted to the tough M.B. and C.M. She knew it would be difficult, but then she had also seen her mother Chandrammal, with an uncommon grit and determination, come out of a system that dedicated young girls as concubines. Muthulakshmi knew that all it took was firmness in belief and action and a kind heart to create new paths.

After she had settled down in the Madras Medical College, Muthulakshmi garnered information about women in medicine. She learnt that the first woman to qualify as a physician in Britain, Elizabeth Garrett Anderson, had to fight and plead for her case too.[3] Anderson had written several letters and petitions, ceaselessly demanding admission to the Royal College of Physicians (RCP). In one letter, Elizabeth wanted only to be admitted to 'some dark and obscure corner' of a lecture theatre. All her requests were rejected but she never stopped asking. She was finally, grudgingly, awarded a lesser licence from the Society of Apothecaries in 1865.

The story of Elizabeth Anderson filled Muthulakshmi's heart with wonder. As women were not allowed to work in British hospitals, Elizabeth founded the first hospital staffed by women, and later became the first woman in Britain to be elected to a school board, and as mayor of Aldeburgh, the first female mayor in Britain. Just her kind of woman! Elizabeth had also joined the society for promoting the employment of women and had organised lectures by another Elizabeth (Blackwell) on medicine as a profession for ladies.[4] Elizabeth Blackwell (1821–

1910)—the first woman included on the Medical Register in 1859, a decade after she qualified in the U.S.—had been rejected by 29 universities.[5]

Mary Scharlieb graduated from the Madras Medical College (MMC) in 1878.[6] She had accompanied her husband William Scharlieb, a barrister who sailed to practise at the bar in Madras. In Madras, Scharlieb learned about the lack of medical services for women's gynaecological health and death during childbirth. This motivated her to gain medical experience, and she wanted to attend medical school. However, her husband did not want her to leave their young family to return to study in England, where women were starting to gain entrance into medical schools. In 1875, she entered the Madras Medical College as one of the first four women students to gain a licentiate in medicine, surgery and midwifery.

Lt A.M. Branfoot of the Women's and Children's Hospital in Madras who was 'not used' to female medical students, supposedly told Mary Scharlieb, 'I cannot prevent you walking round the wards, but I will not teach you.' After graduating, Mary Scharlieb returned to England with her children, old enough by then to travel in a small ship, her eyes fixed on a degree in medicine. Part of her motivation in returning to England was to organise a female-staffed medical service in India. During this period, a medical degree from the Madras Medical College enabled a doctor to register and practise in Great Britain and its colonies. In 1989, British newspapers celebrated the achievement of Mary Scharlieb, the first lady doctor who qualified from the University of London, lauding the fact that Mary had received her primary medical licentiate in Madras.[7]

In 1883, Mary Scharlieb returned to India, and became a lecturer in midwifery and gynaecology at the Madras Medical College and examiner in the same subjects at the University of Madras. She also set up the Royal Victoria Hospital for Caste and Gosha Women, later known as the Kasturba Gandhi Hospital for Women and Children. It was here that Muthulakshmi served as the first Indian woman house surgeon.

Beginning on a path shown by such courageous women, Muthulakshmi knew a challenging time lay ahead of her, but her resolve was strong, and she knew she could work hard as she had the support of her father.

'Is all this history not ironical?' Muthulakshmi asked her father. 'Because women have always been the primary caregivers.' Narayanasami smiled and shared with her what he had read. 'In 1621, Robert Burton wrote in *The Anatomy of Melancholy* that many an old wife or country woman doth often more good with a few known and common garden herbs than our bombast Physicians.' He went on, 'Medicinal recipe ideas have always been passed from mother to daughter with ointments and medicine cabinets that made up "kitchen physic". Women always knew just how to compile ingredients from the garden and the apothecary that was the kitchen cupboard usually.'

Soon, the question of where Muthulakshmi would live came up. There was no hostel for girls at the Madras Medical College then, and those in the city were only for Christian girls. Krishnaswamy Iyer and Dharmambal found a place for rent and helped this family in every manner possible. Muthulakshmi saw that they were progressive in their treatment of girls, and in promoting education as a means of individual freedom.

Her excitement of a new life opening up did take the sting out of a sad news that was received from Pudukkottai. A maternal relative of Muthulakshmi whom she was very fond of had passed away at childbirth. Muthulakshmi remembered that the 16-year-old pregnant girl had bade her a tearful farewell when she left Pudukkottai for Madras. This death made it clear to her that the dedication of young girls as servants of God had to be stopped, and knew she had to fight for it when the time came. Muthulakshmi decided to bring up the baby girl as her own, and named her Subbulakshmi.

It took her some time adjusting to the city. Her father helped her in domestic chores as she was weak and physically exhausted by the great deal she had to study. He took her for walks every day and the conversations they had kept her in good cheer. He always waited eagerly for his daughter in the evenings to talk about the day's happenings at college. If she was late some evenings, he would send a messenger with a lantern to escort her back home.[8]

Madras Medical College had very few girl students then and Muthulakshmi kept to herself. She could afford to buy only a bun from the college canteen for lunch, which she had with a glass of water.

Col. Niblock, the Irish professor of anatomy, and principal of the Madras Medical College was a brusque man but possessed a keen sense of humour, a fund of common sense and a wealth of kindness. Being thorough in all his methods, he was a skillful surgeon, with the faculty of inspiring his patients with complete confidence.[9] Muthulakshmi's steely determination perhaps struck a chord with the Irishman, and she was able to win him over. He began to praise her work frequently. Muthulakshmi did feel the rigour but the effort was not too strenuous, considering her determination to become the first Indian woman doctor to graduate in surgery from Madras Medical College.

Once she had settled down, Muthulakshmi requested her father to bring her younger siblings to Madras for their studies. Ramiah was admitted to the Madras Christian College for a B.A, and her sisters Sundarambal and Nallamuthu to P.T. School (now Presidency High School) in Egmore. Muthulakshmi insisted that her mother bring baby Subbulakshmi with them. Chandrammal brought along a wet nurse for the baby; the household became full, leaving little time for Muthulakshmi to study. The wet nurse turned out to be difficult, and many were the nights when Muthulakshmi studied sitting on the floor with the baby on her lap. She herself was quite sick with asthma, but she dared not complain for fear of her mother packing up and taking everyone back to Pudukkottai.[10]

Some Anglo-Indian student nurses who stayed at the YWCA invited Muthulakshmi to their rooms and spoke to her about the greatness of Christianity, persuading her to convert. Muthulakshmi, however, was more than equal to them, declaring she saw God only in her parents and nowhere else.[11]

There was great pressure from Chandrammal on Muthulakshmi to get married and she had to appeal to her father to come to Madras whenever her mother was visiting Pudukkottai, so that there would be no quarrels on this account.[12]

Her father's visits to Madras were comforting to the young woman who had the daunting task of balancing her medical studies and caring for younger siblings and an infant at home. He cooked for them, and made her morning tea himself, waking up at 4 am to attend to the needs of his children. He sat with his children as they studied after school hours, and nursed them with home remedies when they caught a chill or a fever. He would take their temperature with a thermometer and feel the nature of the pulse. He even had a tiny medical balance at home with powders for emergency use.[13]

Unable to bear the reluctance of her daughter for marriage, Chandrammal went back to Pudukkottai briefly. Narayanasami requested Lakshmi, his elder brother Kuppusami Iyer's daughter-in-law for help in cooking and keeping home for the family in Madras. Lakshmi and Chandrammal had a good rapport and the latter considered Lakshmi a confidante, and always came to her for solace. Lakshmi happily agreed, and moved to Madras for a while, to look after her nieces and nephew.[14]

Lakshmi shared these and many other stories about Chandrammal and Narayanasami Iyer with her grandson,[15] P. Krishnamurthi. Muthulakshmi's younger sister Nallamuthu, the first Indian principal of Queen Mary's College in Madras and a nominated member of the Upper House of the Indian parliament, visited Karaikkudi near Pudukkottai as the chief guest for a function. She had sent word to Lakshmi that she was craving for the delicious *vathakuzhambu* and *suttappalam* (roasted rice wafers) Lakshmi would cook for them in Madras. She came to Pudukkottai after the function to relish it once again. This story was narrated again by Dr Krishnamurthi, Muthulakshmi's son when the two Krishnamurthis met several decades later. Muthulakshmi's elder son Rammohan also had stories about Lakshmi *manni*'s cooking when he visited Pudukkottai, and had gifted her grandchildren one rupee each, a big amount for the children those days![16]

In her second year, Muthulakshmi passed examinations in physiology, anatomy and organic chemistry (considered tough subjects), scoring high marks. She also got her Honours in Biology that year. Examiner Col. Van Geyzel declared Muthulakshmi as the best lady student in the college while giving her the Honours certificate in the selection examination in physics and chemistry.[17]

Muthulakshmi, fascinated by the architecture of the Medical College would wander into the corridors of the Anatomy block situated in the red Indo-Saracenic building. The entire area where the college is situated including the railway station opposite, was actually a small hillock called Narimedu (Fox Hill in Tamil, but also called Hog Hill by some early recorders). When the British built Fort St. George just across the hill, they needed some earth to divert the North river to get more space around the fort. So they decided to flatten the hill and use the earth for this purpose. The medical college had come up on the flat space thus created.[18]

From her third year, Muthulakshmi had to work hard in the hospital clinics, attending lectures in the afternoons. Her first posting for clinical work was under the Irish professor Col. Donovan who discovered the

Kala-azar parasite. He was popular among the students and patients. She enjoyed his classes which were full of humour and fun. An artist himself, he was particularly kind to Muthulakshmi, always appreciating the neat reports she wrote in good English.

She did face some unpleasant bullying and teasing from the fashionable Anglo-Indian students who felt an Indian girl from a small town had no chance in the examinations. This prompted Muthulakshmi to study harder in spite of ill health and asthma. Soon, all the British teachers began to appreciate her work. Col. Donovan would pass around the case sheets she had prepared of patients, and exhibit them proudly to his colleagues. He was the examiner in physiology along with Col. Anderson of Christian College. He is said to have told his colleagues, 'When she entered the hall for the orals she looked very timid and nervous, but when the examiners questioned her, out came the answers like bullet shots.'[19] Naturally, she topped her class.

Col. Giffard, the famous gynaecologist and surgeon, and superintendent of the Madras Maternity Hospital from 1905 to 1917, had high praise for Muthulakshmi when she received several awards and medals at the convocation on graduation. He mentioned, in his speech, that this young woman would inspire other Hindu girls to take up medical studies.

Maj. Gen. G.G. Giffard brought in many changes in the college. It was a time when sulphas and penicillin were yet to be discovered, and doctors had to depend heavily on antiseptic as part of the Listerine era. He built a separate block for the patients who had delivered over 24 hours earlier, and an Out-Patient-cum-Admission block in front of the hospital, and an extension on another side of the main building to form the wings. Muthulakshmi became an extremely reliable house surgeon under Maj. Gen. G.G. Giffard.[20] He called her his right hand.

During Dr Giffard's time, a separate teaching block and hall (that goes by his name now), a museum, an auditorium and accommodation for students also came up. The legendary Dr A. Lakshmanaswami Mudaliar who became the first Indian Principal of the Madras Medical College had said, 'Madras is proud, and justly so, of the place it occupies in the obstetric world of today, and it is no spirit of narrow provincialism that I venture to maintain that no other city in India could have claimed this honour with greater confidence and dignity.'[21]

Dr Mudaliar, who was later knighted, wore many hats—a teacher, administrator, skilled accoucher (one who assists in deliveries) in labour wards, a good surgeon in gynaecology theatres and a brilliant speaker who held audiences spellbound with his mastery over English. He retired to become the vice chancellor of the University of Madras, a post he held for 27 years. During much of that time he continued to serve the Medical Hospital as Honorary Obstetrician and Gynaecologist.

Muthulakshmi and her friends looked forward to Dr Mudaliar's classes. With his moustache and a namam on his forehead, wearing a long white coat and a gold lace turban, he always walked in majestically, with his small entourage. He entered the hospital every morning through a door in the compound wall from his residence next door. From the Cancer Ward, he would make teaching rounds through the Gynae Wards and enter the Labour Ward complex. He would first scrutinise a large birth register and call for detailed causes of each registered still-birth. The students and staff swelled into a big band as they followed him, and the procession was referred to as 'Robin Hood and his Merry Men'. Every case retained for observation in the ward adjacent to the Admission Hall was appraised and he would question the undergraduates, addressing them as 'Doctors', to boost their morale".[22] Dr A.L. Mudaliar was not just a teacher and neighbour to Muthulakshmi but also a good friend and well wisher of her father and was always consulted on all issues of her family.

After the convocation in which she was the star graduate, Muthulakshmi's photograph with the gown appeared in many newspapers. She got several congratulatory letters, including one from the great poet Sarojini Naidu.

Though she began to get offers for appointment from several hospitals, she asked Col. Giffard to give her a place in the Government Hospital for Women and Children in Egmore as she wanted to gain surgical experience under him. He sought permission from the Government to appoint her as there had been no women medical surgeons (officer category) in that hospital earlier. Muthulakshmi became the first house surgeon there. There was resentment from the European nurses in the hospital who were loath to take orders from an Indian girl, but they soon came around knowing she was qualified to do so.

She learnt practical work in Obstetrics and Gynaecology as a house surgeon, and went on to the

Ophthalmic hospital, attending to quite a few cataract procedures under the famous eye surgeon Col. Elliot.[23] This period was not only one for learning the skill of surgery but also for management and administration of institutions, which were to stand her in good stead later.

Narayanasami thrilled with Muthulakshmi's progress, often spoke about her with a sense of pride to his friends. Among those who visited their house and had great conversations about contemporary politics, literature, and the arts was Dr M.C. Nanjunda Rao, a chemical examiner at Madras Medical College and a leading medical practitioner in the city. As a bright student, Muthulakshmi had caught his eye.

It was Nanjunda Rao who opened a great new world to Muthulakshmi. A nationalist at heart and an ardent supporter of the Indian freedom struggle, he would regale Muthulakshmi and her siblings with stories about leaders of the nationalist movement like Tilak, Gokhale and others. He introduced her to the great Tamil nationalist poet Subramania Bharati. Bharati was wanted for sedition by the British and moved around Madras only at night in disguise. He stayed in one of the cottages in Dr Nanjunda Rao's spacious garden for about a week. Dr Rao bargained with a boatman on

Buckingham Canal to take Bharati, who was disguised as a fakir, to Pondicherry, accompanied by the doctor's trusted carriage driver.[24]

Muthulakshmi was awestruck by the splendour of Dr Nanjunda Rao's house on Brodies Road (now R.K. Mutt Road), 'Sasi Vilas' had 16 horse-drawn carriages and an electrical plant for lighting up the house; the women of the house wore diamonds. The household fed nearly sixty people almost every day. Swami Vivekananda visited Sasi Vilas before his tour to America in 1893. Dr Rao made all the arrangements for the marriage of his physician friend Dr Muthyala Govindarajulu Naidu with the young poet Sarojini Chattopadhyay, and it was conducted in his own house.[25] Dr Rao also introduced the Nationalist and poet Sarojini Naidu to Muthulakshmi.

Dr Nanjunda Rao opened a clinic for the poor in Triplicane and named it M.C.N. Eclectic Dispensary. Here, medicines were sold at reasonable prices compared with other places selling foreign medicines. A deeply religious person, he learnt Tamil at an advanced age to study the glory of *Thevaram* and *Thirupugazh*.[26]

Muthulakshmi gradually overcame her timid nature. She listened keenly to Nanjunda Rao's stories. He asked her to contribute articles to his magazine

India, and even invited her to speak at meetings in his house. She was impressed by the humility and sociability of such a wealthy family. He encouraged Sarojini Naidu to take Muthulakshmi along with her to listen to the speeches of Gokhale, to the eloquent, lyrical speeches of Sarojini herself, and to those of other distinguished poets, nationalists, patriots and social reformers. At Adyar, under the great banyan tree, she listened, entranced, to the speeches of Annie Besant, the leader of the Theosophical Society, and her passionate talk about the greatness of the Ramayana and the Mahabharatha.

Muthulakshmi began to frequent The Theosophical Society, fascinated by the gardens with its great banyan tree, and the innumerable birds it attracted, providing the much-needed support to the ecosystem of Madras. She was impressed that the founders had set up the international headquarters on the southern banks of the Adyar river. Founded in 1875 in New York by Madame Blavatsky and Col. Olcott, the society is a spiritual movement that aims to create a universal brotherhood of humanity without distinction of caste, creed, gender or colour. Muthulakshmi was interested in what they had to say, and was impressed with the iconic buildings, the paradise of trees and plants, a library that became a sanctuary for those hungry for research.[27]

Another mentor and family friend Dr C.B. Ramarao, an assistant professor of Physiology at the Madras Medical College invited her home to befriend his two daughters. Muthulakshmi was present at almost all their family functions. He also invited her to women's meetings where she was asked to give her address in Tamil.

P.S. Krishnaswamy Iyer's family had moved to Palathope in Mylapore and they kept in touch with Muthulakshmi and her siblings. Their three sons grew up to be renowned in their chosen fields. K. Swaminathan became a professor of English; he was greatly enamoured of Gandhi after he had been assigned as a young volunteer to look after Gandhi's needs during his visit to Madras in 1915. After retirement he took on the monumental task of editing 100 volumes of the *Collected Works of Mahatma Gandhi*. He was also a devotee of Sri Ramana Maharshi. Swaminathan's daughter Mahalakshmi worked with Muthulakshmi in her social work activities. His younger brother Venkataraman became the Director of the National Chemical Laboratory at Poona, and the youngest Dr K.S. Sanjivi became, not just a distinguished doctor, but also founded the Voluntary Health Services (VHS), a hospital in Madras. The three remained Muthulakshmi's friends for life. All these connections made Muthulakshmi's life as a student rich in diverse ways, providing literary, cultural and nationalist ideas and inputs to her, and contributed to the distinguished path she was about to carve for herself.

Right from her childhood Muthulakshmi was naturally inclined to help children and young women. She would distribute eatables to the children around her house, and was always a popular babysitter. She loved telling stories and listening to the woes of people and gave them a shoulder to cry on. She began to volunteer in the poor areas of Madras doing volunteer health checks on children and girls. As a growing child with weak immunity, constant asthma and breathing struggles, she knew the one thing she needed to campaign for, and put an end to, was the habit among the upper class of hiring women from the lower strata of society to breastfeed their babies. She was herself breastfed by a wet nurse, and this she felt was the cause for the ill health and low immunity in her siblings and her. Education, of course, was on the top of her list—education to help people lead healthy, hygienic and dignified lives.

As promised to herself, Muthualakshmi returned to Pudukkottai to serve her native state after her house surgeonship in 1915. However, the Anglo-Indian lady apothecary and the Chief Medical Officer there created trouble out of sheer jealousy. She decided to go back to Madras, setting up a clinic at No 6: Rundall's Road in Vepery in 1917. Later they moved to Peter's Road in Royapettah. That she became a popular gynaecologist and surgeon and commanded a huge practice is another story.

MARRIAGE AND MORE...

*Where the women are honoured, there the gods
reside; where they remain unhonoured, there
nothing can bear fruit...*

—The Mahabharatha, Anushasana Parva, Ch 46.51

For Chandramma, marriage brought a woman honour. The legal status of a wife and the authority that came with it gave the woman a standing in society and dignity. For daughter Muthulakshmi, however, honour was the independence to pursue a formal education, and the freedom of choice that came with it. Father Narayanasami was caught in between.

It was quite a herculean effort to convince Muthulakshmi to get married. When she went home to Pudukkottai for holidays after her medical studies in 1912, Muthulakshmi's mother consulted an astrologer about her daughter's marriage. He predicted that she would be married in the coming year. The delighted mother promised golden bracelets to the astrologer if it came true, but the daughter was not amused. She was 26 years old and was still not thinking of marriage.

Narayanasami and Chandrammal had long talks with their daughter with the latter tearfully pleading and the former reasoning out. Muthulakshmi told her parents that while she was in the fourth year of medical study, Dr Nanjunda Rao had suggested a marriage alliance with a graduate who had returned from England, but she had firmly declined the offer. Arguing that marriage subordinated women, she spoke about domestic abuse in some marriages. She did not want to be saddled with marriage first as she was embarking on a career in medicine and surgery. Marriage meant motherhood soon after, and all the responsibilities that came with it. Besides, she was already a mother to young Subbulakshmi, the daughter of her young relative who had died at childbirth.

Apart from her medical practice, Muthulakshmi had begun volunteer work at the Young Widows' Home founded by Sister Subbalakshmi.

R.S. Subbalakshmi, fondly called Sister Subbalakshmi, had been widowed at the age of 12. As per the custom, she would have been shunned as inauspicious, condemned to languish in perpetual celibacy, clothed in drab mourning garb, with her head tonsured, confined only to the kitchen as a helper and never allowed to participate in any religious ritual. Unable to bear the cruel fate of Brahmin widowhood that awaited her, her father, Subrahmaniam defied tradition and educated her instead. She was admitted to Presidency School, Egmore, where Muthulakshmi's younger sisters were admitted later. Her parents moved from Saidapet to Egmore as they feared it might be too dangerous for their daughter to travel long distances to the school by herself. Subrahmaniam cycled from Egmore to Saidapet for his work. In 1911, Subbalakshmi became the first Hindu woman to graduate from Madras Presidency. She, along with her aunt Chitti Valambal, also a child widow, got together to take in some young Brahmin widows and help them get an education. Later, with the support of Miss Lynch, the inspector of schools, they were able to upgrade the Young Widows' Home.

It was here that Muthulakshmi had begun to volunteer medical help to the young widows even as a house surgeon. The Home first moved to Mylapore and later to the iconic Ice House, literally used for almost 40 years to store ice brought in ships from North America. Swami Vivekananda, founder of Ramakrishna Mission, stayed here before setting sail for the International Meeting of Religions in Chicago in 1893, to give his famous speech on religious plurality. In 1914 Ice House was bought by the Government and given to Sister Subbalakshmi to run the Widows' Home. Queen Mary's College was just a short walk, and the young women could access higher education easily. Muthulakshmi continued to offer her services as a doctor even after her younger sister Nallamuthu became a member of the teaching faculty, and later the first Indian principal of Queen Mary's College.

Her father assured her if she never married, he would be with her till the end of his life. This statement brought more tears from Chandrammal and more passionate arguments regarding marriage.[2]

It was at this juncture that a letter was received from Dr Sundaram Reddy, L.M.H and the first Indian to qualify for the FRCS. He had heard of Muthulakshmi and her determination to marry only a man who would respect her. He desired to marry her. She replied she was not interested. Dr Sundaram Reddy travelled to Pudukkottai to meet Chandrammal to convince her that he was good enough for Muthulakshmi. He delighted her with family-based sentiments: he would be like a son to her, and he was willing to live with them as his parents had passed away. Finally, Muthulakshmi agreed to meet Dr Sundaram Reddy after her father had met and approved of him. To Reddy's disappointment, Muthulakshmi seemed distant at the meeting. But when he called on her the next day on the advice of a friend, she saw him in a new light as a gentleman, an impression that was deepened subsequently.

Then the miracle happened! Chandrammal was delighted... Her daughter had consented to a marriage! All of Chandrammal's visits to temples, the pujas and the ritual fasting she had done had borne fruit, and her prayers were now answered. Muthulakshmi had agreed to marry Dr Sundaram Reddy.

Sundaram Reddy was a self-made man. His only family was an uncle, Diwan Bahadur Subbaroyalu Reddyar (October 1855–November 1921) of South Arcot, who after his legal studies abroad, had returned to India and got involved in politics. The Government of India Act of 1919, based on the recommendations of Edwin Montagu and Viceroy Lord Chelmsford sought to increase participation of Indians in the administration. Subbaroyulu Reddyyar successfully contested the elections in November 1920 as a member of the Justice Party, and was chosen to be the chief minister of Madras Presidency.

Sundaram Reddy had refused to marry a girl of his uncle's choice, and had left home one night in a classic fashion, with just the clothes on his back, leaving a note behind. He borrowed Rs. 5 from a friend to reach Bangalore (now Bengaluru) and struggled to establish himself as a successful surgeon. To go to Edinburgh for the FRCS exam, he bravely took a loan of Rs.20,000, an astronomical sum in those days.

Muthulakshmi and Reddy were engaged in March 1913, but not before she elicited a promise and an agreement from him that he would respect her as an equal in the marriage, and that he would never object to her social work and other engagements, a promise he kept all his life.[3] Sundaram Reddy gave her a diamond and emerald ring for the engagement.

There was the thorny question of what kind of wedding ritual they would have. Though both Muthulakshmi and Reddy were Hindus, they belonged to different regions and different castes which subscribed to different rituals. They visited the Adyar Library of the Theosophical Society to look up information on marriages, and the rituals involved in the different types of marriages. Ancient texts have described eight types. Of these *Prajapatya* is where the bride is given in marriage to a worthy bridegroom who asks for her hand. This union probably came closest to this mode of marriage, in which the character and disposition of the groom are the only considerations, rather than wealth or material possessions.

Rituals, as they learnt, represented a link between spiritualism and the day-to-day life of the householder, and were derived from the Vedas. Each region of India developed its own marriage rules for each caste and sub-caste, ranging from elaborate rituals to a simple exchange of garlands. In 1868, Keshub Chandra Sen made a petition to the Government of India on behalf of the Brahmo Samaj for a law that would legalise Brahmo marriages.[4] A law recognising civil marriage under Brahmo Samaj was passed in 1872.

They decided to get married under this Brahmo Samaj Act 1872. The groom was perhaps influenced by the ideology of the Justice Party to which his uncle belonged, and the bride by her association with the Theosophical Society. Mesmerized as she was by its President Annie Besant's oratory, and captivated by the ambience of nature and buildings that were in sync with its surroundings, the principles of Brahmo Samaj that the Theosophical Society introduced her to were precious to her.

Muthulakshmi and Sundaram Reddy felt the Brahmo Samaj wedding ceremony was unique in all respects. The founder of Brahmo Samaj, Raja Ram Mohan Roy had aspired to establish a strict monolatrous worship of the Supreme Being.

Muthulakshmi was probably pleased that the Brahmo Samaj did not believe in an auspicious date or time (*muhurtham*) for the wedding, but Chandrammal consulted her astrologer and settled on April 1914. Unlike other Hindu weddings, Brahmo Samaj does not have a *homam* or fire as the witness for the union, but Chandrammal brought a lamp to be lit by the bride and the groom. The wedding was conducted by a Brahmo Samaj Acharya (teacher) and, again, unlike Hindu rituals, the parents of the bride and groom had no role in the ceremony.

A string of jasmine was tied around the right hands of Muthulakshmi and Sundaram Reddy binding them together. These flowers were removed after the marriage vows, when rings and garlands were exchanged. The most significant ritual of any Hindu wedding, i.e., the *saptapadi* or taking the seven steps, was performed but instead of walking around a fire, they took the ritual steps between two lines drawn with flowers on the dais. Each step signified : 1. Paying homage to the Almighty; 2. Promising to co-operate with one another; 3. Promising to cultivate discipline; 4. Promising to discover the source of joy and attain it; 5. For the wellbeing of progeny; 6. For the prosperity of the family; and 7. For the blessing of mutual company.[5]

A large group of medical men and women, including the Surgeon-General of the Indian Medical Services, attended the wedding.[6] They gathered around the couple and showered flowers to bless them. It was an unusual ceremony drawing from the West and the East.

Having made her parents happy, Muthulakshmi Reddy had to now look to domesticity along with her medical practice and social activities. The newly-weds were also burdened with a huge loan.

Sundaram Reddy, tall and handsome, always with a smile had a calming effect on everyone. He was jocular and made light of situations of serious nature that Muthulakshmi was facing on a daily basis as a medical doctor and a social activist, taking on seemingly impossible tasks. His tastes were finer in contrast to her simple Gandhian ways. He gave his wife complete equality in the marriage and looked after her causes with equal enthusiasm.

He was the quiet champion of Avvai Home and looked after every aspect, from finding resources to curriculum, and finding admissions in schools and colleges for the girls to also finding grooms for those ready for marriage. He completely dedicated himself to help the institution after his retirement as the first Indian head of the Anatomy department of Madras Medical College. There were many legal issues involved, and it was Sundaram Reddy who sat with the lawyers. Muthulakshmi began to earn much more than him as she was in private practice, while as a professor in the Government college, he was not allowed private practice. 'If his ego was hurt, he never showed it,' said Krishnamurthi, his son.

On Narayansami's suggestion, Sundaram Reddy accepted the post of Chief Medical officer in Pudukkottai. Chandrammal was delighted that her son-in-law would be working in a prestigious post in her hometown. There was the promise of a good salary and great appreciation of the public who soon recognised Dr Sundaram Reddy as a conscientious and skilled surgeon with a keen sense of duty. Dr Reddy's frequent travels around Pudukkottai on medical emergency calls, and the relentless stream of patients all day took a toll on his own health; he developed high fever and moved to Madras to be cared for by Muthulakshmi. After being treated for pyorrhea and getting a tooth extracted, he recovered and returned to Pudukkottai. Though the work was strenuous, the atmosphere was comfortable for Dr Reddy in Pudukkottai. He had a bungalow for himself, a car and half dozen helpers in the house.

Muthulakshmi stayed back in Madras as she had already established a busy practice, while continuing her social work. She was also expecting her first child. Through her pregnancy she worked round the clock, till the day she went into labour. World War I had broken out, and there had been some arguments in the house; an upset Muthulakshmi had not slept all night when she developed the pains. She had to endure a long and difficult labour of seven days.[7]

Chandrammal could not believe labour could be so difficult. She had given birth eight times and each one had been an easy delivery. Having literally forced her daughter to marry, she took the blame on herself, and threw away all her jewellery crying that she would kill herself for putting her daughter through this ordeal.

Muthulakshmi's brother Ramiah sat in another corner praying loudly for his sister's life. Narayanasami swore he would renounce worldly pleasures if something should happen to his daughter.

23 December 1914. The medical attendant gave Muthulakshmi an injection of pituitrin despite her protest.[8] The pain became excruciating and went on for four more hours, while Muthulakshmi screamed in agony, asking for chloroform. The membranes had ruptured but the head of the baby was high in the pelvis. Dr A.L. Mudaliar, who was her neighbour, attended on her and applied forceps while Muthulakshmi was under chloroform. The doctor looked for a perforator to pull out the baby, at least to save the mother's life. But the perforator had not been sterilized. By the time Dr A.L. Mudaliar came back with the sterilized perforator, Rammohan had been delivered and was howling as loudly as any newborn; both mother and son were safe. It was a new world. Muthulakshmi was overjoyed, even though the baby was premature and weighed only 3 pounds. In her autobiography, Muthulakshmi attributes the wellbeing of her first born to Dr A.L. Mudaliar's timely intervention, and praises him as a conscientious and able obstetrician.[9]

The difficulty experienced by Muthulakshmi brought about a short rift between Chandrammal and Narayanasami Iyer. He stopped visiting Chandrammal's house, setting the whole town talking. If she had continued her maternal family tradition, Chandrammal would perhaps have composed a musical piece about her man not visiting her anymore, wondering if he was seeing someone else. But Chandrammal had left that life behind. She would stroll every day to Narayanasami's family home where he lived with his brothers and their families, regally walk to the backyard, pick up some vegetables growing there and saunter back home, her head held high. Tongues wagged of course. 'When he has stopped going to her house how can she pick vegetables from his garden?' She was actually doing this to ascertain her right as his partner. This was her husband's home as far she was concerned. The affection and regard for Chandrammal in Pudukkottai grew multifold after the two reconciled. An amazing act of courage at the time and circumstance she was living in.[10]

Rammohan was just three weeks old when Muthulakshmi travelled to Pudukkottai, on 15 January 1915 to join her husband. He was a delicate baby and had to be wrapped in a shawl and carried by a male nurse who kept awake through the overnight train journey.[11] Pudukkottai was proud to have an FRCS from Edinburgh as their Chief Medical Officer. Such a highly qualified person had not served in the district before.[12] Dr Reddy, in his official capacity and in his private practice, attracted the attention of not just the poor in Pudukkottai, but also quite a few important Chettiars and Zamindars in the district around. Several successful cases made him popular. His fame had spread by word of mouth. Patients began to arrive in droves to consult him.

Though there were quite a few mortalities, many patients made dramatic recoveries which were termed miraculous by their families. There was the instance of a young man gored by the bull he was handling in a *Jallikkattu* event. His stomach was ruptured and his intestines were visible through the gash in the abdomen. He was wrapped in a wet cloth and carried into the hospital by his friends. Dr Sundaram Reddy attended on him in his usual meticulous way. When the young man recovered, his entire village came to thank him, bearing gifts of agricultural produce in gratitude. Muthulakshmi was no less busy with some extremely difficult pregnancies and deliveries. She also began to attend on urgent cases as there was no alternative medical aid for the women and children in Pudukkottai.

The couple had their hands full. Their list in the operation theatre was long and they worked continuously. He travelled as far as 40 miles to attend on patients for which he was rewarded handsomely, gradually paying back the loan he had availed of for his education.

Pudukkottai afforded a luxurious lifestyle as the house was right next to the hospital,with nurses and friends ever eager to help. There was an abundant supply of milk, and grateful patients, rich and poor, brought fruits, vegetables and other goods as gifts for the family.

Muthulakshmi breastfed her baby even after her family strongly recommended she should wean it. She believed that a mother must give the natural nourishment of her milk to her baby as long as she could till she is unable to do so.[13] Rammohan's health picked up. However, for Muthulakshmi there was hardly any rest.

The physical and mental pressure on the couple mounted. Dr Sundaram Reddy developed rheumatism owing to lack of proteins. He fell ill frequently with high fever that would sometimes make him delirious. Dr Muthulakshmi Reddy called for medical help from

Madras but none was forthcoming as most of his friends were busy with their practice. Dr Sundaram Reddy's student arrived to help at the clinic, but all medical decisions had to be taken by Muthulakshmi herself.[14] Rammohan developed whooping cough and suffered a great deal in the nights, causing his mother great anxiety. She had never seen such suffering. Her sister and she lay on either side of the baby at night with a thermos flask of warm water to wet his throat before he got into a paroxysm of cough. After four weeks a *vaidyan* who practised indigenous medicine suggested that the baby could be given an ounce of fresh toddy in the morning and evening. Muthulakshmi was willing to try anything. They noticed some relief, after three days the intensity of the cough gradually reduced. Muthulakshmi writes in her autobiography: 'Whether it was due to this treatment or due to the natural waning of the virulence of the disease, we do not know. However, we carried the impression it was due to the administration of fresh toddy which contains yeast. When he was a year old, before he got ill with whooping cough, I began to learn Sanskrit letters from one of my old professors in the college who was an M.A. in Sanskrit and very proficient in teaching. I learnt to spell Sanskrit words. I asked for help in reading Sanskrit medical texts.' This coming from an allopathic doctor shows the open-mindedness she brought to her profession, as much as she did to her personal life.

On recovering from his fevers, Dr Sundaram Reddy resumed his duty, tackling office work, operating room experiences, the business of medicine, anxiety over anesthesia efficacy and much more, while Muthulakshmi was living the life of an obstetrician. Each day was punctuated with true, unfiltered experiences, funny, joyful, fearful, and tearful, that can only be found in the life of an ob-gyn surgeon and an anatomy surgeon.

The couple never lost sight of their aim to help others find their feet and live a healthy life. Dr Sundaram Reddy provided several allowances to the sub-assistant surgeons by granting grade salaries to new men, and enhanced salaries of the attendants, the cleaners and the support staff. All this was noted with a tinge of jealousy by the palace officials, and he had to put in considerable efforts to implement them.

Dr Sundaram Reddy was also anxious to find his own feet, independent of the palace intrigues and contemplated leaving Pudukkottai as he had some misunderstanding with the administrator of the hospital and the Diwan.

While in Madras on a visit, Dr Sundaram Reddy got to know that a vacancy was coming up in the Madras Medical College for an assistant professor. After just a year-and-a-half of service in Pudukkottai, Dr Sundaram Reddy and Muthulakshmi decided to get back to Madras. Muthulakshmi's parents were shocked that the couple was willing to give up such a good medical practice with all the accompanying comforts and conveniences of a chief medical officer. However, a decision had been made and they were given an affectionate send off, with a heartfelt speech praising the couple.

Life in Madras was not very easy. The household was large since Muthulakshmi was shouldering the responsibility of educating her younger sisters and brother, adopted daughter Subbulakshmi and her own sons. The Reddys missed the luxurious life of Pudukkottai. Everything was expensive in Madras. In Pudukkottai, fresh vegetables, fruits, fish, eggs and fowls were gifted by grateful patients. Here everything had to be purchased. The cooks, gardeners, peons and attenders who had served the couple most loyally in Pudukkottai were all in the employment of the state. One of the attenders had decided to follow the couple and helped in looking after Rammohan, but other help had to be hired. Rented houses had to be frequently changed to find the most comfortable one. A horse-drawn carriage was required, besides a cook, an attender, a driver and a domestic help. All had to be fed thrice a day besides being paid a salary.

Dr Sundaram Reddy had been nominated as the assistant professor of anatomy at the Madras Medical College, but the service rules did not permit him to have private practice. So it was that Dr Muthulakshmi picked up her own medical practice where she had left it. Her practice increased manifold but her baby also kept her awake at night.[15]

When Rammohan turned four, the couple decided to conduct his *Vidyabhyasam*, a ritual to mark the beginning of formal education. Dr Muthulakshmi wanted to mark the day by feeding the children of Dr Varadappa Naidu's Home for Poor and Destitute Children. On one of her visits to the home, she was appalled by the unhealthy appearance of the children and the insanitary conditions in which they lived. She decided to visit the home regularly and suggest remedies but these ideas were not accepted initially by the management. Later Dr Sundaram Reddy was chosen as the secretary of the home. He collected Rs.4000 from his patients in Chettinaad and constructed a compound wall.[16] After she became the Deputy President of the Madras Legislative Council, Muthulakshmi was able to get some of her proposals implemented.

Muthulakshmi was now expecting her second child and suffered nausea, becoming very weak. Her mother who was barely fifty years old passed away suddenly from an attack of pneumonia. She had been preparing to go to Madras to attend to Muthulakshmi's second delivery. Muthulakshmi was unable to travel to Pudukkottai for the funeral due to her pregnancy, and had to endure intense grief without the close family support she needed.

In 1919, M.K. Gandhi declared a passive resistance hartal at a speech he made on the Marina beach in Madras; over 1000 people had died in Jallianwala Bagh; Chandrammal's death shocked her, a raging influenza epidemic infected Dr Sundaram Reddy and sister Nallamuthu. In the midst of all this, the birth of her second son, Krishnamurthi on 12 September 1919, brought a lot of joy to the family.

Muthulakshmi was examined by her professor Lt. Col. Giffard through her pregnancy, and Dr A.L. Mudaliar was there all night to attend to the delivery. This time it was an easier delivery, but there was an unexpected difficulty. The newborn's eyes were rinsed with a solution of cleaning fluid instead of sterilized water, by mistake by the attendant, causing them to swell dangerously. All the lights in the room were immediately covered with green paper and the superintendent of the Ophthalmic hospital was called in to treat the baby's eyes. Dr Muthulakshmi Reddy writes in detail in her autobiography about the two deliveries, and the illnesses in the family, for the benefit of future mothers.

Though Muthulakshmi was earning around Rs 3000 a month from her practice, considered quite lucrative for those times, she was always running short of funds, which was not surprising given Dr Sundaram Reddy's expensive tastes. Further, the large household of children and staff was increased by the hordes of relatives and friends dropping in unannounced from Pudukkottai. Musicians and dancers from out of town were always greeted warmly by Muthulakshmi, and their needs catered to even when she was not at home.

Dr Sundaram Reddy would often jest that he had little privacy in his own home.

The couple was experiencing all the trials, tribulations, joys, and fears of married life, tensions of financial management and parenthood while working round the clock. Through all of these, they learnt everything about the human condition which prompted Dr Muthulakshmi to find more time for social work to bring about changes in the situation of countless women.

THEATRE OF LIFE

Nothing in life is to be feared, it is only to be understood. Now is the time to understand more, so that we may fear less.

—Marie Curie (1867–1934)

Fearlessness was the cornerstone of Muthulakshmi's life, a quality she had imbibed from mother Chandrammal. It was this fearlessness developed painstakingly, that energised and awakened her. She was able to bravely take on with ease, not just a medical career, but also combined it with motherhood, simultaneously working on myriad pioneering social reforms. Muthulakshmi became one of the most influential women in education and healthcare in the Madras Presidency, and saved countless lives. The institutions she founded continue to do so.

Among the first things she began campaigning for was to change the system of wet nursing that had been a matter of prestige among upper class families.

A woman who could afford it, hired a woman from the economically lower class to breastfeed her newborn. Muthulakshmi and her siblings had been breastfed by wet nurses. She felt this was the reason for her ill health as a child. Even as a medical student, she had made up her mind to address this issue of parenting.

As a doctor, she examined and treated adolescent girls who had torn membranes, a sign of violent intercourse. Most of them were frail and suffered from malnutrition. They had several miscarriages as their wombs were not strong enough to retain the foetus to full term. Repeated occurrences made the girls anaemic and weak, and many of them developed tuberculosis. It was no surprise that there was a high rate of young girls dying during childbirth. The husband married again, and the new bride, perhaps even younger than the previous one, was expected to take care of the motherless infant and brace up for her own delivery.

This relentless cycle was nauseating for Muthulakshmi, and she agonised over it. In her autobiography, she cited the case of a 12-year-old, married to a man aged 40 who had lost three wives. He consummated the marriage even before the girl attained puberty. Muthulakshmi pleaded with the husband to have some patience but he would not listen. No one was surprised when a year later the girl also died at childbirth.[1]

Muthulakshmi had seen young widows at Sister Subbalakshmi's Sharada Illam where she served as an honorary medical consultant. The two women had a lot in common, born in the same year 1886, and dying within a year of each other—Muthulakshmi in 1968 and Sister Subbalakshmi in 1969. Both served as members of the Legislative Council of the Madras Presidency, though at different times. When the philanthropists of Mylapore objected to admitting non-Brahmin girls in the Young Widows' Home or the school they went to, Muthulakshmi decided that when she would establish a home for girls and a school, it would be for all castes.[2]

Both women were hands-on in their management of their institutions and their practice. For instance, Sister Subbalakshmi noticed the girls were finicky about food, having been accustomed to eating the left-overs in their homes. She complained to Muthulakshmi who made a nutrition chart for the girls and insisted they eat greens and grains every day.

The two women also shared a deep belief in the power of education to change women's lives. Sister

Subbalakshmi's efforts were aimed at getting the young widows an education and campaigning for their remarriage. Muthulakshmi felt the answer to problems with early marriages lay in the education of the girls.

Sister Subbalakshmi was an educationist by every definition of the word. Her students at the P.T. School in Egmore wept copiously when she bade them good bye before moving the widows to the Widows' Home in Mylapore. She founded several educational institutions all over the Madras Presidency. In 1920, she set up the Kuppam School, later renamed Lady Willingdon High School, near Ice House so that it would be within easy reach of the children of the fishermen who lived near the beach. In 1927, she established Sarada Vidyalaya, which was later handed over to the Ramakrishna Mission. The last institution she established was Vidya Mandir in the heart of Mylapore.

As the eldest, Muthulakshmi had taken on the responsibility of educating and looking after her younger siblings, besides her two sons and an adopted daughter. Her values were shared by her siblings. When the girls in the sixth form at the P.T. School were asked to write an essay on what they thought should be the next step forward in the education of Indian girls, Muthulakshmi's younger sister Nallamuthu won the prize for her essay in which she had pleaded for a college for women in Madras.[3] A few days later, a member of the governing Executive Council for education was visiting the school, and Nallamuthu was asked to read the essay in his presence. He was impressed but skeptical about any Indian girl wanting to spend around five years studying in a college. When he jocularly asked how many girls in the room would want to go to college, every hand went up. Madras Women's College was set up the following year in 1914. The name was changed to Queen Mary's College in 1917. Nallamuthu studied and also taught there, and went on to becoming its first Indian principal. Most girls from the Widows' Home graduated from Queen Mary's College and found their vocation.

Muthulakshmi kept abreast of all the socio-political events and changes being brought about in the country. In 1913 she met Lady Whitehead, who was organizing a social service league to improve the conditions of women and children in the slums of Madras. Muthulakshmi became a member and gave free consultations to women and children in the slums.[4]

The Theosophical Society, taking cognizance of the interest of girls in education and social emancipation, decided to form the Women's Indian Association (WIA) to bring women together for mutual assistance. Annie Besant, Dorothy Jinarajadasa, Kamaladevi Chattopadhyaya, Margarette Cousins, Muthulakshmi Reddy and others were involved in its activities of promoting the education of girls, equal property rights for women and the advancement of the age of marriage of girls. Equal voting rights, reservations in legislatures, the de-linking of women's franchise from their marital status, and a non-discrimination clause were part of their demands. For those times, these were remarkable and bold articulations of constitutional arrangements that were intended to protect and promote the rights of Indian women.

Muthulakshmi was the first Indian member of the Women's Indian Association (WIA) and also served as the editor of its journal *Stri-Dharma* for many years since its first publication in 1918. Although predominantly an English publication, this journal was multilingual, with sections in Hindi, Tamil, and Telugu. The in-house journal, whose name could be translated as 'Sphere of Women,' 'Women's Duty' or 'Justice for Women,' aimed to become the voice of the Indian women's movement.

One way the 'woman question' was addressed was through channelling public opinion. Women began to use journals such as *Stri-Dharma* to give women's issues and consequently the Indian women's movement a voice. *Stri-Dharma* established its own role in informing the public on issues of employment, health, and education,[5] including child marriage, divorce, purdah system, women's property and inheritance rights and the physical health and wellbeing of Indian women.[6]

Muthulakshmi agreed totally with the WIA that India would gain in power for good if it developed a woman's side to its activities. She believed freedom and independence had to be given equally by law to women as changing the social customs and attitudes would be slow and difficult. Then women would at least have the recourse of law if they found the courage to fight the situations they were in. It was through *Stri-Dharma* that the demands of the WIA linked to the constitutional future of India were made. The journal put forward particularly important goals and principles of a future constitution:

1. Women should be free to contest seats in the general constituencies, subject to the same qualifications to apply as men.

2. In addition to any seats thus secured by women, a certain proportion of seats—say 5 per cent, as suggested by the Nair Committee—should be reserved for women in each provincial council, at least for a trial period of three general elections.

3. Reservation should be filled in any suitable way that may be determined by the next Round Table Conference.

4. Full adult franchise is secured for both men and women. Any woman—married or unmarried—possessing any one of the general qualifications for the franchise would have the vote.

In 1917, the Montague Chelmsford Commission for constitutional reforms was touring India. A WIA delegation met the Commission and argued that women be given the franchise. Many men opposed this and the Commission rejected the demands, but the WIA did not give up, and made the demand for equal voting rights a focus of its work.

Throughout 1917, WIA intensely lobbied and established relations with major political groups in India and convinced them on the question of voting rights for women. The Indian National Congress, its many committees, and the Muslim League regularly passed resolutions in their annual session to remove disqualifications for women voting, and this issue was incorporated into the formal constitutional demands directed at the British by all the parties. This wide-ranging support group with a consistent agenda was lauded as a momentous achievement for the WIA.[7]

When the Southborough Commission came to India in 1918 to review the question of franchise among other things, the WIA went all out and leveraged the organisational machinery it had built. In cooperation with other women's organisations, it demanded equal voting rights for women. But the Commission felt the social conditions in India were too premature to extend the vote to women, and dismissed WIA's demands. WIA came up with powerfully articulated critiques of British policy on the franchise for women, and laid bare British hypocrisy in the letters to the government and in articles in the press, persisting with its demand for equal rights. WIA pressed for a bill of Rights that included rights to freedom of expression, non-discrimination and more. Importantly, it contained a fundamental right that aimed at sex discrimination: *There shall be no disqualification or disability based on gender.* Muthulakshmi Reddy clearly explained the need for these reforms in her powerful speeches.

Another issue the contributors to *Stri-Dharma* continually argued against was the 'crime of infant marriage.' Why should they be denied the freedom and education that would allow them to grow into 'strong, happy, educated, and free young men and women?' WIA pressured politicians to support the bill, their delegations holding placards and shouting slogans such as 'If you oppose Sarda's bill, the world will laugh at you.' It was also this group that pushed for, and eventually succeeded, in having Gandhi address the evils of child marriage in his speeches. Victory for the bill can be credited to the WIA, which presented the Act as a means for India to demonstrate its commitment to modernity.[8]

Muthulakshmi collected some data to support the demand to increase the age of marriage for girls.

Table 1

Married Women and Widows in the Madras Presidency in 1926

Age	Married	Widowed
0–5 years	20,369	1,316
5–10 years	1,23,472	6,146
10–15 years	5,37,206	23,623
15–20 years	11,76,063	60,544
20–25 years	17,69,587	1,57,026
25–30 years	16,55,732	2,23,384

An interesting aspect of WIA and *Stri-Dharma*,and their focus was that they looked at fighting the battle for the new idea of womanhood, not only in the public sphere but also at home. The inner space of the middle-class home served as an important focal point for 'the history of women's issues.' The home became the battlefield for women's rights. It is within the sphere of the home that the issues Indian women faced on a daily basis were most evident.[9] The status of women at home became a primary colonial justification for the colonizing mission and served as the basis for its argument regarding India's political readiness.

By 1920, as the WIA increased its profile and popularity in Madras, Muthulakshmi spearheaded efforts to establish a woman's home as Indian Ladies Samaj and a baby welcome centre in Mylapore. Within a year, 9200 babies were brought to the centre, where they were bathed in clean water and given medical aid, and their mothers were advised on diet and hygiene. Muthulakshmi rendered honorary service at both these centres.

The strategy of bringing the home front into the public sphere was apparent in the efforts to raise the age of marital consent. Muthulakshmi worked within the WIA to pass the Sarda Act, named after its sponsor Har Bilas Sarda. Despite strong opposition from the British authorities and orthodox men, the Child Marriage Restraint Act was passed on 28 September 1929 in the Imperial Legislative Council of India. The Act fixed the age of marriage for girls at 14 years and boys at 18 years, later amended to 18 for girls and 21 for boys. While the Act was a necessary first step for the health and wellbeing of adolescent girls, its enforcement was one of the biggest challenges the reformers faced. The first problem was the reporting of underage marriages. Those who were courageous enough to report those in their community who were violating the Act, were then forced to pay a deposit before the authorities would investigate the claim. Another challenge was presented, when despite warnings, the marriages took place or the families evaded the law by performing the marriage outside British India.[10]

Despite taking on these responsibilities Muthulakshmi did not lose sight of her large household. She conducted the marriage of her younger sister Sundarambal with a Maratha youth who was an artist from Rabindranath Tagore's Santiniketan. He had been trained as a sculptor in London on a Tagore scholarship, and was employed at the School of Arts in Bangalore. This story, however, ended on a sad note. Sundarambal was a happy, expectant mother in Bangalore till she found some droplets of blood in her stools. Muthulakshmi looked after her sister for over a month. She sat up nights, praying for hours for her sister's relief from suffering. Sundarambal passed away in 1923, with her sister by her side. Devastated, Muthulakshmi vowed to work on cancer care.

Two years later, in 1925, she got the opportunity. The Raja of Panagal helped Muthulakshmi get a Government of India scholarship to go to England for

11 months for postgraduate study in diseases of women and children. Muthulakshmi needed a break from her extremely busy medical practice, so she decided to take her husband, adopted daughter Subbulakshmi and sons Rammohan and Krishnamurthi, along with her to London. Nallamuthu had already secured a scholarship to study at the London School of Economics.

Muthulakshmi set sail for London, entrusting all her property and belongings to her brother C.N. Ramiah who was now an advocate at the Madras High Court. He was active in anti-caste movements and travelled to many villages to settle disputes between the upper classes and the oppressed. While on one such mission, he was chased by the police and was injured, trying to escape. The wound turned septic and proved fatal.[11] There was a public meeting and procession to bemoan his loss.[12] Muthulakshmi learnt of his passing on reaching England, and this following so closely on her sister Sundarambal's death left her devastated. Adding to the sorrow was her inability to attend his funeral.

The sea voyage of the Reddy family had its own adventures. Eighteen-year-old Subbulakshmi became seasick, retching and vomiting. She also cut her finger severely while doing a chore. Though Muthulakshmi sutured it carefully, the scar remained for years.[13] Her 11- and 6-year-old sons and husband had their own issues, the least of which was spending a considerable sum of money on drinking water at Rs.1 to quench their thirst. It was cold on the ship and their cotton clothes hardly kept them comfortable. Since their warm clothes had been sent ahead, they had to bear their suffering.

Their arrival in London was a series of mishaps. Their train from Marseilles reached Victoria station very late, on a dark and rainy night. By that time, their friends who were supposed to receive them had returned home. The whole family, with their luggage, crammed into a taxi, and headed to Nallamuthu's boarding house. It was a hostel for students, not families, and their room was on the third floor. To top it all off, the food was decidedly unappetizing, with only cold fish and meat to eat.

Settling into a new environment was a challenge. Finding suitable accommodation was difficult. In fact, many boarding houses the couple approached had a discouraging notice stuck on the door: No children allowed.

While Rammohan got used to the different diet and conditions, Krishnamurthi wanted comfort food like curd rice, buttermilk and pepper rasam. He fell ill so often on account of the cold climate that his parents seriously considered moving him to warmer climes like Southern France. Fortunately, he got accustomed to London, and gradually improved.

Though manners, customs and civic rules were completely different in England, the family found plenty to delight them. While Rammohan was in the hospital for phimosis surgery, the nurses would visit him in his ward as they had never seen a young Indian boy. The children were highly amused that the British changed their clothes before every meal. Muthulakshmi found shopping in London relaxing, and was amused that her own proficiency and eloquence in English astonished her British peers.[14]

All three children were admitted to a school in London so that their education would not be disrupted. English governesses looked after them in the evenings when the parents were busy in the hospitals. Muthulakshmi was happy that it was safe for the children to take long walks in the parks by themselves; the British were kind and considerate towards them.

The Irish maids at the boarding house became fond of the family and allowed Muthulakshmi to use the kitchen where she could cook Indian dishes on Sundays.

Muthulakshmi was impressed with the famed formality of the British, and their disciplined ways. When she was involved in an accident on the escalator in an underground station, a stranger bodily lifted her to safety, and walked away before she could thank him sufficiently.[15]

Once when Dr Sundaram Reddy travelled with the children on the underground train, he got off first at West Hampstead station, however, the train moved on before the children could get down. The other passengers averted an accident by holding on to the children who were ready to jump off the train to join their father. Dr Reddy called the next station and the authorities reunited the family promptly.

As a patient in hospital, she noticed the way it was run through voluntary services, and appreciated the civic sense displayed. Muthulakshmi underwent surgery in London for amputation of the cervix by the expert surgeon Victor Bonney. She had already been through a similar procedure in India, but a correction to rule out malignancy was necessary.

While in London, Muthulakshmi received an invitation to visit Paris to take part in the International Congress of Women. The best and foremost of women from around the world were there to deliberate on the problems of the world's womanhood. Delegates from 42 countries exhibited a deep concern for the status of women. She observed the commonalities of issues across the world, that the needs of women in every country, whether East or West, were the same. She noted that everywhere women had grievances of some kind or the other, and suffered persecution, injustice and inequality of treatment.[16] Muthulakshmi was impressed with the paper presentation of Dr Paulina Luisa of Uruguay on 'Equal moral standard and against traffic in women.' She felt it bore testimony to Uruguay's intellectual attainments, capacity for research and perseverance after truth and justice. Muthulakshmi also enjoyed her visits to the Sorbonne University, Pasteur memorial, Napoleon's palace and to various hospitals, and met several members of the French elite.

She also represented the WIA at a meeting of the International Women's Suffrage Alliance, which stood for the progress of all women without distinction of race or religion. She reported that the WIA, at that time, had 61 branches, and over 3000 members in India. A majority of men were favourable to women taking on an active role in the affairs of the country. However, the average age of an Indian was 25 and the percentage of educated men around nine, and that of women less than two. She reiterated her view that only education would bring home the truths about ignorance, poverty, insanitation, and was intent on establishing free and compulsory elementary education through the length and breadth of India.

The Reddys sailed back to India through Ceylon.[17] She was reminded of her brother whose wife was born in Ceylon, and relived her grief at losing him. A small ship brought them across the Palk Strait to Dhanushkodi from where they took the train to Madras, where a huge reception awaited them at the station. At a meeting organised in her honour, later that evening by the WIA, she gave a comprehensive speech describing her experiences in London and Paris.

Now back in Madras, she had to resettle the family and attend to multifarious things such as the arrangements following her brother's death, school admission for the children, and setting the house in order. A pleasant surprise awaited her. WIA had sent the names of women they wanted to nominate to the legislature, and Muthulakshmi's name was the second on the list after Kamaladevi Chattopadhyaya.

Dr Muthulakshmi Reddy entered the Madras Presidency Legislative Council as a nominated member for the first time on 14 December 1926. She was the first woman to become a member of a legislative council in India. On 24 January 1927 she was unanimously elected deputy president of the Council, becoming the first woman in the world to hold such an office. Congratulatory messages poured in from women's organisations all over the world. Receptions were held everywhere and invitations to speak at public meetings and conferences piled up. There was much research and study to do in preparation, before she could begin piloting bills and resolutions in the Council for social reform, education and health of women and children.

Her vast exposure to people of different cultures and her experience as a doctor in the intimate issues faced by women gave her a personal philosophy of an unusual depth and breadth. She acquired a spiritual side expressed in her love of knowledge, search for solutions, refinement and concern for the poor, self-discipline and understanding of the deepest hopes, fears and aspirations of women. She believed the authentic vehicle of civilisation was the consciousness of ordinary women who were beginning to value and demand the rights to make their own choices, organise their lives, choose their occupations and enjoy life without a sense of guilt.

WIA began to take an active part in all the negotiations between Indians and the British. Muthulakshmi was chosen to represent Indian women at the International Congress of Women in 1933 and travelled on the ship *Berengaria* to New York. Being the only Indian, she was conspicuous in her sari and was received warmly by the Americans. The press was interested in whether she knew, and was a friend of Gandhi. Next came queries about caste in India, untouchability, child marriage and the political situation. Her photographs were published in the newspapers with 'additions and exaggerations.' To be more prepared for these stock questions, she decided to write down her answers. She attended a party given by Lady Rockefeller, enjoyed the tour around New York and Central Park, and marvelled at the magnificent new church facing the river and the exquisite music played on the large church organ.

She met up with the Dutch, Italian, Romanian, Syrian, Swedish and Danish delegates and took the train to Chicago with them. At the conference, she was introduced to many prominent women of the disarmament committee, members of the League of Nations and of the National Council in Chicago. In addition to the lectures and the discussions at Congress Hall, there were parties, dinners and entertainment in honour of the distinguished guests. Her speeches on creative citizenship and the woman's role in it were a big hit, an experience she described in great detail in her autobiography.

Muthulakshmi visited the Chicago exhibition which she thought was magnificent, showcasing the achievements of intellect and skill in several spheres of human activities like education, health, science, trade, commerce, art, traffic and transport, machinery, architecture, painting, sculptures and music. Her bordered saris were admired, and once while she was standing near the gate of the Congress Hall, a flower seller approached and gifted her a bunch of flowers as a mark of appreciation of her sari.

There were more trips abroad representing Women's Indian Association at the Round Table Conference in London in 1934.[18] Her reports on her trip to Burma as a member of the Hertog committee on education reform, and to Ceylon where she studied the plight of Indian women labourers in the plantations there, were praised for their precision. She wore several hats—as a doctor, mother and social worker, and now as a legislator, a role she performed with her usual exactness and thoroughness.

YUGADHARMA AND CREATIVE CITIZENSHIP

•────────────────────────────────•

For Gandhi, every community has to deal with the
perennial problems of human existence as reflected in its
specific and changing circumstances. What is to be done
for the time is yuga dharma. It had no other way to find
answers to them except by the method of trial and error.

—Bhikhu Parekh[1]

Mahatma Gandhi got up from the cotton mattress he was seated on as she entered the hall. He came up to her, embraced her and asked her how she was going to serve the women. Kasturba Gandhi was standing nearby. Muthulakshmi met Gandhi in 1927 at the Mowbray's Road residence of S. Srinivasa Iyengar, freedom fighter, and a leading member of the Congress party. He and his family were patients and friends of Muthulakshmi. His daughter Ambujammal founded the Srinivasa Gandhi Nilayam where the ashes of the Mahatma are kept under a tulsi plant. Muthulakshmi showed Gandhi the bill for the protection of young girls and women which she wanted to present in the Legislative Council, and sought his blessings. He declared he was in full agreement with the main object of the bill. He later expressed his full support by writing about it in his publication, *Young India*.[2]

The period between 1926 and 1930 was politically and socially intense for Muthulakshmi. A new anti-colonial national identity was being forged in India and it was struggling to make its name in the world. Women were challenging the traditional roles to which they were confined. Formal education system had opened its doors to all castes. Skill-oriented and hierarchy-driven workers were aspiring for a new horizon that might liberate them. Large feudal landholdings were getting smaller with the younger generation moving to the cities in search of modern vocations. In the midst of it all, Muthulakshmi was questioning and attempting to radically redefine, deconstruct and reconstruct the orthodox conception of womanhood in India, and relate it to contemporary times.

Muthulakshmi agreed with Gandhi that every tradition was a resource, a source of valuable insight into the human condition and part of a common heritage. Gandhi's statement 'I do not want my house to be walled in on all sides and my windows to be stuffed. I want the culture of all lands to be blown about my house as freely as possible. But I refuse to be blown off my feet by any' appealed to her. She believed it was essential to learn about one's own religion and recommended religion to be taught in schools.[3]

Gandhi's words and views were of great encouragement and strength to her. According to him, the basic values and insights of a tradition were valid and binding because they had survived the rigorous test of lived experience and scrutiny of their critics. Every society was articulated at two levels and its basic values and insights, its central organizing principles had an enduring significance whereas its beliefs and practices were subject to constant revision.[4]

Muthulakshmi organised a large meeting for Gandhi at the Hindu High School Triplicane on 31 August 1929 under the auspices of the Women's Indian Association. A purse was presented to the Mahatma by the women for his work, which, he joked, was of course, not enough. Muthulakshmi also travelled with him to the southern parts of the Madras Presidency, and translated many of his speeches into Tamil as he spoke. Gandhiji's child-like simplicity and open-heartedness, and his ready support to a measure of a controversial nature during that time, made an indelible impression on Muthulakshmi's mind. After that meeting, she did not hesitate to write to him whenever she felt she was in need of support for her reform measures in the council,[5] and she was assured of his full support.

After Muthulakshmi and her family returned from the UK in 1926, she become a member of the Children's Aid Society for sheltering and protecting vagrant children picked up by the police. Along with Mrs Stanford, a theophist, she organised several institutions, such as Senior and Junior Certified School, Boys and Girls clubs, Juvenile Court and Remand Home; this gave her the opportunity to come in contact with destitute, delinquent and mentally challenged children, and with minor girls who had been sexually trafficked.

The Madras Legislative Council was set up in 1921 under the Government of India Act 1919 following the recommendations of the Montagu-Chelmsford Reforms for representating the government in India with legislatures comprising elected representatives of Indians. The term of the Council was for a period of three years. It met for the first time on 9 January 1921 at Fort St. George, Madras. In the 1926 election,

C.V.S. Narasimha Raju was elected the president of the Madras Legislative Council. The election of the Deputy President of the Council took place on 24 January 1927. In April 1926, the Government of India allowed women to contest elections and sit along with men in the legislative councils. All the parties decided to nominate Muthulakshmi Reddy, whose name was proposed by a member of the Justice Party P.T. Rajan (22 April 1892– 25 September 1974), and passed unanimously.

Muthulakshmi was aware that as a member of a legislative body under British rule she had a platform to express her views and act on them. Both she and Sister Subbalakshmi decided they would not get into the freedom movement through protests and hartals, though they supported the struggle. She was not daunted that the reforms she was seeking to involve herself in required immense administrative work. As a member of the legislative council, she kept her association with WIA and AIWC alive, and continued her involvement with the Sarada Home, Women's Home of Service (now called Madras Seva Sadan) and the Society of the Indian Ladies Samaj for the protection of minor girls. She was an active member of the Madras Maternity and Child Welfare Association, and worked for the opening of the health school. She was also one of the founders of the Muslim Ladies Association.

In 1926, as the deputy president of the Madras Legislative Council, she devoted a major part of her speeches pleading for a special children's hospital, for the extension of compulsory medical inspection in girls' schools and for sanction of special grants to women's institutions, for the appointment of women medical officers in hospitals and for a women police force. She stressed on the evil effects of alcoholism in families, and supported prohibition. Almost every question she raised in the Council was a matter affecting women and children. She pleaded against separate electorates for women and for different castes, and advocated for amendments to the Madras Children Act to make provisions for prevention of punishments for child offenders. She studied the publications of the League of Nations and other relevant material for her campaign for reform, and was well prepared for all the questions she was being asked by the law makers, the general public and more particularly, the press.[6] She was supported by most modernists, but some nationalists and many Hindu and Muslim conservatives opposed the concept of government interference in religious matters like age of marriage and the purdah system. Marriage laws remained under the authority of the religious texts of each specific religion.[7] However, both the WIA and the AIWC to which she belonged, appealed to and took along with them, women of all religions. Women were confident that this combined energy would remove one of the main stumbling blocks to female education, and hence facilitate fuller participation of women in the political and social life of the emerging nation.

Muthulakshmi believed that education would put girls in a position to get rid of the chains that bound them.

In 1927, the director of Public Instruction in Bengal called upon Indian women to 'tell us with one voice what they want' in terms of education. This was widely reported in the press. Margaret Cousins followed up an article on this speech in the WIA organ, *Stri-Dharma* with letters to the WIA branches. She appealed to women all over the country to form local committees and hold Constituent Conferences for voicing their views on problems of education, 'From each of these conferences, representatives should be elected who would attend an All India Women's Conference in Poona.' She wanted this conference of 'not more than 40 to 50 women' to synthesise from the proceedings of the preliminary conferences 'an authoritative and representative memorandum by women on educational reforms.'[8]

When the All India Women's Conference (AIWC) was formed in 1927, and eventually registered in 1930 under the Societies Registration Act XXI of 1850, the founders recognised that they would have to discuss social as well as educational issues. The delegates met in Poona to discuss the larger issues. When they discussed female education, they emphasised the difficulty in separating this issue from those social customs which denied women access to education. Before long it became obvious that these issues could not be separated from politics and the AIWC, along with other organisations, began to discuss Indian nationalism as well as 'women's issues,' refusing to identify themselves as feminists. They did so as they were not putting women's rights before those of the nation, and were not anti-men, nor did they view men as the enemy.[9]

Muthulakshmi agreed with close friend, the poet and freedom fighter Sarojini Naidu who had developed a model with India as the 'house', the Indian people as 'members of the joint family', and the Indian woman as 'mother'. Child marriage, seclusion and prohibitions against schooling prevented women from playing this role. For the women of the 1920s and 1930s, it was clear that only freedom from restrictive customs would make it possible for them to contribute to the regeneration of India.[10]

The Hindu Child Marriage bill introduced in 1927 was the first social reform issue which was taken up by the organisations of women in India. The AIWC and WIA mobilised women to lend their support to an issue they had recognised from their inception as a detriment to female education and health. They played a major role in the development of the argument and actively used the device of political petitioning and in the process contributed to the field of politics.[11]

Muthulakshmi wanted women to own responsibility, not just for begetting children and keeping a home, but to also have an enlarged role in society. She believed that a progressive government with liberal values would always adhere to the progress of all. She wanted to use the power that her education and her position bestowed on her to exercise autonomy and choice wherever possible.

On 8 November 1927, the British appointed a Statutory Commission under the chairmanship of Sir

John Simon, to examine the working of the Montagu-Chelmsford Reforms, implemented on 23 December 1919. Restricting the appointment of all members of the Commission to members of the British Parliament was considered a great insult to the Indian sense of self-respect. There was an immediate outcry in the country and the entire nation rallied to Gandhi's call for boycott of the Commission when it arrived in India on 3 February 1928. Wherever the Commission went in Indian cities, it was greeted with black flags with 'Simon Go-back' slogans. The Indian press voluntarily came forward to report the weaknesses of the Simon Report and openly condemned the anti-Indian attitude of the members of the Commission. The political literature treated the outcome of the report as just 'eye wash'.[12]

The influential Tamil newspaper *Swadesamitran* in its issue dated 19 February 1929 remarked: 'The members of the Commission arrived in Madras yesterday like *gosha* ladies. Their condition is indeed pitiable. A few persons were presenting an address of welcome to the Commission at the harbour, while thousands of people were taking part in the boycott activities. It is not clear what right a few members of a certain class have got to present an address of welcome on behalf of that class.

If Sir John Simon and his colleagues should think that such addresses are presented by the people they should indeed be fools.'

Annie Besant joined in the boycott and the Congress and its allies all joined too. Muthulakshmi followed suit. One of the several organisations and auxiliary bodies of the government appointed to assist the Commission's work was to study the educational progress in India. Muthulakshmi was invited to serve on the committee to focus on women's education, and though she was boycotting the Simon Commission, she did not want to lose a rare opportunity to undertake an in-depth national study on education. It probably also helped that the chairperson of the committee Sir Philip Hartog, Vice chancellor of the newly created University of Dhaka, was considered a great educationist. Muthulakshmi was impressed with his sympathetic attitude, not just for women's education, but also for the right of Indians for self-government. He was also favorable to women's aspirations for more and better education, and equal rights and equal opportunities. The secretary Sir R.M. Stratham, Director of Public Instruction of Madras Presidency, also had great sympathy for the women's cause.

Muthulakshmi's understanding of girls' education expanded exponentially as the Hartog Committee visited several institutions imparting education to girls. She was delighted to get first-hand knowledge about the progress of women's education in every state of British India including Burmah (now Myanmar). 'It was not only interesting but also highly instructive as I came in contact with every quarter of the country, both purdah and non-purdah areas. Even in the states where Purdah was observed there were highly educated and intelligent women among them who conducted girls' schools." she observed.[13] Muthulakshmi was given cordial receptions wherever the group went, and girls and women assembled in large numbers to hear her.

The report of the Hartog Committee, submitted before the Simon Commission in 1929, holds a unique position in the history of Indian education. It tried to feel the pulse of education in India and made practical recommendations in regard to primary secondary, higher and also some other aspects of education. It greatly influenced the educational policy of the British government since the report was looking at consolidation rather than expansion.[14] The Committee observed that there was considerable progress made in education by that time. In general, people regarded education as a matter of national importance as signaled by increasing enrolment in primary school, indicating that the sense of indifference to education was breaking down. Women, Muslims and the backward classes had also awakened and there had been rapid progress in the numbers. However, the Committee was not satisfied with the growth of literacy in the country.

The report was the first official recognition of the neglect of primary education, and blamed the provincial governments for poor progress of primary education. It pointed out that the problems of primary education were basically rural, and it drew attention to the problem of wastage and stagnation. The Committee argued for qualitative improvement. Regarding secondary education, the Hartog Committee laid emphasis on industrial and commercial subjects, thereby making provisions for the students to take up practical vocations in life. The Committee praised the growth of affiliated colleges but criticised the falling standards of university education and was firm in its opinion that the universities had failed to meet the needs of the people. It was the duty of the universities to produce such individuals who were tolerant, liberal and suitable to undertake great responsibilities. Developing the libraries of the universities was one of the important recommendations of the Commission.[15]

Finally, the Committee distinctly remarked that qualitative improvement of education was not possible unless the conditions of the teachers were improved.[16] It recommended improving the pay scale and service conditions of the teachers, and rightly stated that no education could be successful unless the teachers were well paid and enjoyed the security of service. Unfortunately, the government did not choose to implement the recommendations on the teachers.

Meanwhile, the debate about raising the age of marriage for girls was raging. Muthulakshmi moved a resolution in the Madras Legislative Council that was unanimously accepted. The AIWC arranged a deputation to the Viceroy Lord Irwin, and public meetings were arranged all over the country. Thus, the Child Marriage Restraint Act actually helped to solidify the connection between the women's movement and the nationalist movement.

Muthulakshmi Reddy gave evidence before the M.V. Joshi Committee in Allahabad, enquiring about the raising of the age of consent and marriage. Gandhiji had given his whole-hearted support to this demand, 'I am strongly in favour of raising the age of consent, not merely to 14, but to 16. Therefore, I should heartily endorse any movement whose object is to save innocent girls underage from man's lust.'

On the other hand, there were severe criticisms against the bill for meddling with religion. Muthulakshmi's resolution placed her in the middle of a huge storm, and there were heated exchanges in the assembly. But Muthulakshmi was firm. She insisted that any practice observed for some years would become a custom. When a law member Campbell argued that this was not like *sati* which was a more heinous custom, she flew into a rage and argued sharply that child marriage was even worse, because it was lifelong suffering for the girl. The reply left Campbell dumbfounded, and he refrained from criticising her resolution further.[17] She toured rural areas to speak at public meetings on the issue and met with hostile crowds at some places, even being pelted with stones by some miscreants.[18] But she took everything in her stride and she, too, began to use strong language to reply to her critics. The Child Marriage Restraint Act, 1929 was passed on 28 September 1929, in the Imperial Legislative Council of India fixing the age of marriage for girls at 14 years and boys at 18 years. It is popularly known as the Sarda bill, after its sponsor Har Bilas Sarda. It came into effect six months later, on 1 April 1930, and applied to all of British India.

Another area of women's welfare Muthulakshmi studied was the brothels in the city that were facilitating the trafficking of girls. She wanted minor girls to be removed to safe places and the perpetrators punished. Her bill introduced in 1927 for Suppression of Immoral Traffic of Girls had lapsed. Muthulakshmi introduced a bill in 1928, seeking punishment for those who participated in the vice for gain. The bill was referred to a select committee, and the Suppression of Immoral Traffic Act was finally enforced in 1932. Later amendments to the bill reflect that Muthulakshmi had clearly stated that those who were rescued must not be jailed but sent to rescue homes. In 1954, she moved for the inclusion of a clause for a woman welfare worker specially trained, to accompany the police whenever they entered a place where women were being trafficked.

By 1933, the Vigilance Association got over 123 brothels closed, and the rescued minor girls were sent to Children's Aid Society and Seva Sadan. WIA set up a rescue home known as Ananda Villa in 1934. Muthulakshmi, in her welcome address, said that the home was to receive and protect girls and women rescued from brothels, to provide for their moral and spiritual welfare, and to educate and train them to help them stand on their own feet. To the numerous questions whether the homes were really providing for their welfare or restricting them and whether prostitution could ever be totally eradicated, Muthulakshmi retorted that along with the existence of evil, honest attempts should be made to alleviate human suffering. 'We are responsible for the evils we tolerate and for those we do not resist actively,' she thundered.

In every petition of hers, Muthulakshmi demanded that all laws should be equal for men and women, and both should be made equally responsible for any offence committed by them together.

The person who contested and argued against Muthulakshmi for her bills was erudite scholar and orator from her town Pudukkottai, S. Satyamurthi. Born in 1887, just a year after her, he had studied in the same college but was a conservative to the core. Just like her, he had moved, after his Intermediate in Raja's College in Pudukkottai to Madras. He studied history in the Madras

Christian College, and then went on to study law. His political career started in 1919 when he was made the secretary of the Congress delegation that went to the Joint Parliamentary Committee in the UK to protest the Montagu-Chelmsford reforms and the Rowlatt Act. In 1926, he was again sent to the UK to present the Indian point of view to the British public. While he was there, he was also the London correspondent of *The Hindu*. In 1940, he was arrested for taking part in the freedom struggle, and died in 1943 of a spinal cord injury suffered in prison.

The press supported Muthulakshmi's bill and during the debate, she had to compromise on one aspect and cede on another. She wanted to redefine the word 'prostitute' as without male chastity, women's chastity was not possible, and so wanted both men and women to be brought under that definition[19]. But the men protested, and finally, the House agreed to define prostitution as 'indiscriminate sexual intercourse for hire.'

The clause to punish the third parties was dropped; hence the victims became the accused most of the time, and the perpetrators, by virtue of being men and having some high connections, were always let off. This deletion upset Muthulakshmi even though she received high praise for her achievement. To compensate for this deletion, she pressed for more women police officers for the safety of women.

She did not confine her gaze only to issues in India. As a legislator, she visited the plantations in Ceylon and looked at the conditions of the Indian labourers there. Speaking in Tamil to the labourers, she enquired about where they had come from and why they were working in such unfavourable conditions. She made a detailed study on their education, health and financial situation, and made a report suggesting specific improvements. She took up their cause in her addresses to the All Ceylon Women's Association, Buddhists Association, Muslim Association and the YWCA.

In 1930, Muthulakshmi resigned from the Madras Legislative Council protesting the atrocities by the police on Satyagrahis during Mahatma Gandhi's Salt Satyagraha and his imprisonment. She was holidaying in Ootacamund (now Udhagamandalam) when the news of the arrest was received. She immediately announced her intention and within an hour her letter of resignation, both from the Council and the deputy presidentship, were in the hands of the governor.

In recognition of her meritorious services in the Council. Muthulakshmi was given a public reception on 31 October 1930, at the WIA headquarters. A congratulatory address signed by prominent citizens of Madras was presented to her by Ammu Swaminathan, a social worker and a member of the Constituent Assembly of India. Muthulakshmi was hailed as someone who utilised her time at the legislature to the fullest benefit of women.

It was no mean achievement to be the first woman in the Legislative Assembly and to push so many bills and debate with brilliant orators such as S. Satyamurthi and C. Rajagopalachari, particularly to defend her bill for raising the age of girls at marriage, against immoral trafficking of women and against the dedication of young girls as Devadasis. As a reformer, she worked to question the rationale of unacceptable practices and to expose their irrationality, simultaneously exhibiting contrary approaches and emotions, sympathetic understanding and critical spirit, patience and indignation, in her opposition to these issues. 'The decision,' writes her son Dr Krishnamurthi, 'as to her next step (after resigning from the Council) was a very difficult one to take. There were three alternatives, i.e., to return to the very large and lucrative medical practice that she had before becoming a legislator; to enter politics; or to continue follow up action on the many social reform laws that she was responsible for enacting.'

She was in the middle of discussions with her husband and her father at her Madras home when three young girls running away from the Devadasi system knocked at her gates. The decision was taken out of her hands. Establishing Avvai Home and an educational institution for them became her next preoccupation.[20]

THE DEVADASI QUESTION

*Any art or culture worth preserving will certainly hold
its own against all times and against all conditions. Our
attempt should be to free it from its ugly associations and the
incrustations of ages which now keeps it dim and repulsive
to many so that the divine art may be learned by all ... then
only India's art, the rich legacy of ages, will shine brighter and
will command respect and admiration of the world.*

—Dr Muthulakshmi Reddy[1]

Muthulakshmi was concerned that the word 'Devadasi' was considered as an abusive term in Tamil. She wanted to release women born to Devadasis from the curse, and give them a future free of such an association. If dance and music were so integral to the system that so oppressed a woman, they must be halted too, so that new art could emerge.

Reams have been written about the Devadasis, their mores and customs. Several researchers have discussed the system as an awe-inspiring source of traditional music and dance, that the Devadasi was a

Nityasumangali (one who never became inauspicious as she would never be widowed, because of her marriage to the eternal God), that she had sexual freedom, and enjoyed the privileges not available to ordinary women. Why then did Muthulakshmi 'go after' the Devadasi?

Her maternal relative Saimata Sivabrindadevi (1927–1998), the first woman head of the monastic order of the Pudukkottai Thilakavadhiyar Adheenam, (daughter of Sivarama Nattuvanar and a sister of mridangam artist Tirugokarnam Ranganayaki) wrote in a letter to the editor of *Sruti*, the music and dance magazine 'My maternal aunt Dr Muthulakshmi Reddy revealed great anguish she felt because in those days it was common to abuse a girl of any community even for using cosmetics, by asking her rhetorically, "Why do you make up like a *Tevadiyal*?" Applying facial make up was not solely the custom of the Devadasis, but the abuse directly or indirectly pointed towards them. A real Devadasi maintained a code of conduct and was choosy in selecting a man as her common law husband, but when once she did it, she spent her entire life only with him. The meaning of the term *Devaradiyal* came to be corrupted and misused in a nauseating manner. My *Periamma* (elder aunt) Dr Muthulakshmi Reddy agonised over this state of affairs and resolved to remove the stigma attached to the Devadasis. This was the real reason for her moving the bill. None need think that it was a move to protect members of this community from immorality; there was really no basis to think of it in this manner, because, barring a small number, all other were more than chaste housewives. On many occasions, *periamma* explained this to me: Good and bad people will be found in every caste and community. Prostitution was not the monopoly of any particular community. Immoral traffic had become—and is today-a hobby or luxury or even a profession among many in all communities.'[3]

'In its early years, the thirties and forties of the last century, when the British ruled the country, their focus was economic and political control of the area to ensure British prosperity. Social changes were studiously evaded under the guise of neutrality in the country's religious affairs. Even the Devadasi Act was enacted amidst total governmental indifference,' writes Muthulakshmi's son Krishnamurthi.[4]

The term Devadasi, *devar adiyar* in Tamil, is derived from two words meaning God, *devar* and servant or *adiyar,* of. They were women who had been ritually dedicated to a deity in the temple. They served in the temple and their duties included fanning the deity with *chamaras*, (fans made of Tibetan oxtail hair), and carrying the sacred light of *kumbharathi*. They possessed the right to sing and dance before the idol during certain times of worship, or when the deity was taken out in procession on the main streets. The temple provided accommodation and a modest remuneration. Along with the male members who sang, conducted and choreographed the dances, they developed the art forms to a high level.

The employment of Devadasis by temples has an ancient history. According to the inscriptions at Rajarajeswaram (later Brihadeeswara) temple in Thanjavur, over 400 Devadasis were transferred from various other temples on the occasion of its inauguration in 1010 CE by the powerful Chola king Arulmoli Varman, also called as Rajaraja. Young girls were donated, recruited or purchased for temple services to pacify the wrath of the gods and pray for the bestowal of graces and goodwill: perpetuation of the queen's marriage; longevity for the king; the welfare of princes; an army commander seeking spiritual merit;[5] and parents fulfilling their vows by dedicating a daughter.

Dedication to sacred service was done irrespective of caste and social considerations; in one case, a princess voluntarily dedicated herself to a temple, for which her father gave away much of his wealth as dowry.

On the account of their marriage to God, Devadasis were *nityasumangalis*. A mortal girl would have to remove the mangalasutra and was considerd inauspicious or *a-mangali* in case of her husband's death, and would be excluded from all ritualistic events. The Devadasi was believed to live in a permanent state of auspiciousness, a cause for envy among married women, and possibly also fear. This also allowed the Devadasi to be invited to wedding ceremonies, where her presence was sought to remove the effects of the 'evil eye' caused by jealousy, and to bless the bride and pass on some of her auspiciousness.

Many Devadasis had a single patron all their lives, who supported her family, according to his whim and fancy, with gifts of funds or produce from his fields. However, the the children born out of this relationship could never be legal heirs or claim any inheritance, not even his name; all such privileges were accorded only to his legal wife and her children. It was predictable that the Devadasi would be stigmatised as a home-breaker.

Ancient Tamil literature described women as innately possessing certain traits such as *achcham* or timidity, *naanam* or coyness, *madam* or innocence and *payirpu* or chastity, and an aversion to men who were not their husbands. However, these traits were not necessary for a 'public woman' who attracted men with her music, dance and youthfulness. Several scholars maintain that a Devadasi cannot be called a *paratthai* (the other woman or prostitute in Tamil) as the former was necessarily dedicated as one while the latter was not.

Two women had showed the steely determination displayed by Muthulakshmi in her fight for the abolition of the system in the face of stiff opposition. The first was her mother Coviloor Chandrammal and the other was Muvalur Ramamirthammal.

Coviloor Chandrammal went against the customs and traditions of the family she was born into when, at the age of 11, during the rituals of her *Bottukattudal* (dedication), she had held the hands of her much older patron Narayanasami Iyer and had declared, 'You are my husband. I will be loyal to you all my life. Please make a home for me and take me away from here. I do not wish to continue the custom of my community.' Narayanasami had been a reluctant patron at her Bottukattudal ritual.

He was not a rich landholding zamindar materially able to support a Devadasi and her family. As the principal of H.H. Raja's college and a tutor at the palace of the Raja of Pudukkottai, he was a salaried man with limited means. He had the respect due to his learning and his association with the palace, since it was the king's sister who was asking him to be the official patron at the *Bottukattudal* of Chandrammal, he felt there was no way he could refuse.[6]

When Muthulakshmi turned six, Chandrammal's brother and uncles came to discuss her future. They were angry with Chandrammal for not following the protocol (*murai*) ascribed to the women of her community. Little Muthulakshmi was witness to the courage her mother displayed as she stood at her door like one possessed and refused to go back to her mother's house. 'I am ending the Bottukattudal ritual with myself, and I want to get my daughters married. They will not become public women,' she had thundered. The gossip mills had worked in hushed tones of envy and respect at the audacity of the young woman. They knew she had the support of her patron Narayanasami and he in turn had the support of the local royalty, even if the palace officials were jealous of the respect and affection he commanded.[7]

Chandrammal was known to be an extremely strong person who spoke in no uncertain terms about anything she saw amiss. She was also a noble and extremely helpful person and kind to all those she interacted with. Chandrammal brought up her daughters in strict discipline, hoping to prepare them for marriage. But her first daughter, inheriting her streak of rebellion, rejected marriage and saw education as the redeeming factor.[8] Chandrammal constantly fought with Narayanasami arguing for marriage which she felt was the only way to gain respect for a woman.[9] She wanted their father's name for her children, which was never the case for the children of other girls in her community, who carried the name of their mother's native place. Thus, Muthulakshmi and her siblings used the initial C.N. (Coviloor Chandrammal, Narayanasami Iyer).[10]

Muvalur Ramamirthammal (1883–1962) was introduced to Muthulakshmi by E.V. Ramaswami or Periyar when he was in the Congress. (Erode Venkatappa Ramasamy, also known as Periyar or Thanthai Periyar, was a social activist and politician, who started the Self-Respect Movement and Dravidar Kazhagam. He is known as the 'Father of the Dravidian movement') Ramamirthammal had been working at the grassroots for changing the Devadasi system of dedication of young girls. Periyar felt Muthulakshmi's ideological position on woman's education and freedom, and her position as a member of the law-making body, would help Ramamirthammal's movement.

Muvalur Ramamirthammal was born in Tiruvarur in 1883. Her father Krishnaswami belonged to the Paravai Natchiyar lineage of Devadasis of Tiruvarur. His dedicated sisters, who did not have children, wanted to adopt his daughter, but he, like Muthulakshmi's mother, was keen to let his daughter have a different life. He left for Muvalur, where his wife Chinnammal had family. Unable to get any employment due to the caste restrictions there, Krishnaswami abandoned his wife and daughter and ran away to Madras where he got a job as a garden sweeper in a rich household.

Driven by need, five-year-old Ramamirtham was sold by her mother to a Devadasi called Aachikannu for the princely sum of Rs. 10 and an old sari. Fearful of the little girl's reaction, the tearful mother left Ramamirtham when she was asleep, and escaped to join her husband in Madras.

She was brought up with love and care by Aachikannu. A quick learner, Ramamirtham became quite proficient in music, Telugu and Sanskrit by the time she was 10.[11] When she was seven, her training in dance began with the appropriate ritual of *Gejjepuje.* Paddy chaff was spread on the floor, on which she was asked to stand by the dance master. Two women held a staff between them and she was asked to hold it with both hands. Her master held her ankles and made her stamp on the chaff in time to the syllables he recited. He was given fruits, clothes and gifts at the end of the session.[12] When Ramamirtham attained puberty, she was given the formal name Muvalur Ramamirthammal though she was born in Tiruvarur. A formal debut performance of dance was planned, a practice known even in the ancient Tamil epic *Silappadikkaram.* This practice permitted, as was the case with the courtesan Madhavi in the epic, that the companionship of a young dancer, after she had performed publically for the first time, could be bought by a patron. Her subsequent fate depended on many factors. In later times, a girl who had been dedicated to a temple through the ritual of *Bottukattudal* had to be prepared for the man to abandon her at any time, and she needed all the skills she could muster to keep him devoted to her.

The Agama shastras, rules of worship, prescribe certain age limits of the new entrants for the marriage to a deity. According to *Kamikagama*, (ancient text of guidance for personal worship and conduct), a Rudraganikai (one in the hierarchy of Devadasis) should be married to the deity between the age of seven and nine at a ceremony to be solemnised on an auspicious day and time. The Acharya, who had already observed the necessary fasts, should alone conduct the ceremony. After strict observance of the vows, the girl is seated in front of the sanctum sanctorum. The Acharya unties the *talibottu* (sacred pendant on a turmeric drenched thread) from the deity and ties it around the girl's neck, thus solemnizing her marriage to the deity. A chosen patron from among the aspirants would have the rights to be the girl's companion for the duration he wished. Girls were expected to give cash and other gifts as dowry to the deity as an obligation. This expense was mostly born by the designated patron. A seal made of copper or silver bearing the deity's symbol was heated and pressed onto her upper arms to mark her perpetual bondage to the temple, making it impossible for her to leave the temple service. If the girl were to be employed in a king's palace, his symbol was branded on her arms.[13] There is a legend that when a king returned some Devadasis to the temple they belonged to, the symbol of the king had to be erased from their arms and replaced with the symbol of the temple. An ordeal by fire.[14]

Aachikannu decided to conduct Ramamirthammal's *Bottukattudal* and dedicate her to deity of the local temple when she turned 17. An application for the ceremony was made to the trustees of the temple in Muvalur but it drew opposition from the Devadasis who were already working at the temple, on the grounds that Ramamirtham was not from Muvalur. Aachikannu then planned to get Ramamirtham married to a 65-year-old man who claimed to have fallen in love with Ramamirtham, and said he did not want a dowry. Ramamirtham panicked and decided to take things in her own hands. She ran to the temple looking for her music teacher Suyambu Pillai and asked him to marry her. He was troubled, 'Your *gejjepuje* has been done. You have held the *danda* (staff for training in dance) and have already sung in public. How can I marry you? Even if we get married will society accept it?' Yet he was willing to make her his life partner. (He already had a wife and children in his village.) They went to the temple at Vazhuvur, lit the lamp promising each other lifelong togetherness. The only witness to this was the trustee of the Muvalur Margasahayeswar temple, Velu Padayachi.[15]

Aachikannu did not approve of this marriage and threw Ramamirthammal out of her house. Enraged orthodox persons made several attempts to disgrace the couple, even going to the extent of foisting a trumped-up case of the murder of a young girl on Ramamirthammal, but were foiled when the 'victim' appeared dramatically at the trial in court.[16] Ramamirthammal and Suyambu Pillai remained steadfast in their support for each other.

During this time, a young girl from Madurai had come to meet Suyambu Pillai. Listening to her sing, he predicted a great future for the girl.[17] It was M.S. Subbulakshmi, who, like Coviloor Chandrammal and Muvalur Ramamirthammal, later took an independent decision to renounce her connections with the Devadasi system. In an interview with journalist and author Vaasanthi, M.S. Subbulakshmi had said, 'There was so much pressure on me, I just wanted to get away from that atmosphere.' So, at 19, she took a night train all by herself and landed at the house of T. Sadasivam who, by creating a protective golden cage, controlled every minute of her existence after that. 'Music was her passion. Sadasivam gave her the opportunity to sing. She thought it was to her best advantage to go by what he said. I really feel it was a strategy she decided upon,' says Vaasanthi.[18] Sadasivam managed her singing career to such an extent that she was awarded the Bharat Ratna, the highest honour India could bestow upon a civilian. His total control over her is a matter of much analysis and public discourse, but she remains one of the most loved singers of India.

These two women, Ramamirtham and Muthulakshmi, were taking their lives in their hands, stunning their surroundings with their determination and hard work, and were about to embark on a mission to change the lives of other girls in society.

In Muvalur, Suyambu Pillai agreed with his wife that women's liberation was equal in importance to political independence. He was already influenced by Gandhian ideology and looked for respect and dignity as the very basis of life. The couple earned their living by teaching music and languages. Since Ramamirthammal knew Sanskrit well, she could explain the meanings of the *sloka*s (Sanskrit verses) and discuss them with girls from the Devadasi community. Though she had disapproved of Ramamirtham's marriage to Suyambu Pillai, Aachikannu bequeathed her wealth and house to her adopted daughter. Ramamirtham was able to bring her parents back to Muvalur. The couple organised the first major conference to discuss the abolition of Devadasi system in Mayavaram in 1925. It was Ramamirtham who renamed Melakkarars as Isai Vellalar, as those who make a living by sowing the seed of music and dance in the culture. She and her husband visited villages and towns, speaking in support of the Devadasi Abolition Bill of Muthulakshmi.

The Madras Hindu Social Reform Association was formed in 1892 to promote the social status of women. The Association sent memorandums to the Governor-General and the Government of Madras Presidency to put an end to the practice of dance being performed at private and public functions in which British officials also participated.[19]

By the turn of the century, kings had lost their powers, first to the East India Company and later to the British. Huge land holdings and the zamindari feudal systems slowly disintegrated. Men from smaller towns flocked to Madras, the seat of power and trade, in search of education, employment and opportunities. These migrants carried with them their cultural memories and preferred to hold on to laudatory rather than oppressive memories. Honouring and patronizing the Devadasi system was difficult for them in these new circumstances. This was further reinforced by women whose access to education empowered them to be able to question polygamy.

Muthulakshmi travelled all over the Madras Presidency and participated in several conferences on the subject. Muvalur Ramamirtham wrote in her notes that she felt like a lone voice in the wilderness to get the Devadasi system abolished, but when Periyar introduced her to Muthulakshmi, she was thrilled to find a kindred spirit who could also use her position to bring about a legal solution.

While she fought for women's education, right to property, voting rights for women, widow remarriage and raising the age of marriage, Muthulakshmi brought forward a childhood wish to do right for her mother. She had observed the way the Devadasi girls were treated by their patrons and the general public. As a doctor examining young girls, she had noted the poor status of their health and how susceptible they were to diseases She wanted to put an end to it.

In 1926, Muthulakshmi gave a notice of resolution against the Devadasi system to the government. This bill was the culmination of long deliberations and discussions with the women from the community.

Many were with her, while some protested vehemently. She named it, the Amendment of the Madras Hindu Religious Endowments Act. She wanted an immediate end to the dedication of young girls to 'immoral vicious life'. She believed that the immorality associated with the Devadasis was inconsistent with the Hindu tradition, past and present, and that the Devadasis should disassociate themselves from the temples. The bill proposed that lands controlled by Devadasis contingent upon their temple services be handed over to them, and detached from the service requirements. If a Devadasi was entitled only to a portion of the revenue from the land, she should continue to receive this income without being obligated to perform any service.[20] She said that both state and religion should guard the morality of the people rather than regulating, licensing or sanctifying vice.[21] She tabled the Devadasi Abolition Bill in the Madras Legislative Assembly in November 1927 after discussing it with Muvalur Ramamirthammal and Periyar. Her arch-rival in the Assembly, veteran Congressman S. Satyamurti stated that the women from the Devadasi community were the sacred safety valves and essential to society. A much publicised, though apocryphal story is that Muthulakshmi retorted that if he felt so concerned about it, he should let the women from his family be Devadasis. There is no record of this exchange anywhere, but Jeevasundari in her biography of Muvalur Ramamirtham claimed it was Ramamirtham who was the voice behind these words. It is possible that the verbal exchange did take place and was deleted from the records.[22]

Muthulakshmi's son Krishnamurthi was witness to the preparations his mother made during the debates. 'I have seen my father Dr Sundaram Reddy and Dr C.R. Reddy, an uncle who later became Sir C.R. Reddy, the founder of Andhra University, rehearse my mother over and over again for the next day's debates in the Legislative Council, with the gentlemen acting as the opposition. None would ever know that some of my mother's triumphant retorts in the Legislative Council were often conceived in my father's brain. Father never demurred in mother's actions.'[23]

In a written response in the magazine *Revolt*, Muthulakshmi used strong language to explain her position on the Devadasi question. 'Of all the laws, rules and regulations which down the centuries have helped to place women in a position of inferiority, none has been so very powerful in creating in the minds of men and people a sentiment of scorn and contempt for women as the degrading idea of the double standard of morals.'[24]

She thundered, 'From this double standard that has sprung that worst attack on women's dignity, that safety valve theory that a certain number of women should exist, should sacrifice their self-respect, their honour, their comforts, their health and happiness to satisfy the lust of the other sex. At the present day, the continuance of such a doctrine and of the laws which are founded on it, is a shameful anachronism unworthy of our civilisation.[25] Both in the past and in the present, women have disproved their inferiority, and how then can we at the present day tolerate or connive at a system which transforms a woman of whichever caste or class she may be, into a mere chattel, a piece of tainted merchandise? The inequity of the system is too deep for me to give expression, and further under that inhuman and unjust system the innocent children of a certain caste or community are trained to become proficient in all the arts of solicitation that they become captives to vice.'[26]

There was a huge campaign to counter this bill by some conservatives and those who supported the system. Muthulakshmi had to bring all the resources at her command to counteract this propaganda. The WIA was solidly behind her. She published articles in the press and distributed pamphlets. The associations which supported Muvalur Ramamirthammal invited Muthulakshmi to preside over their meetings. The great Nadaswara Vidwan T.N. Rajarathnam Pillai completely supported Muvalur Ramamirtham to have the system of dedicating young girls abolished. On 8 July 1927, a special conference in support of the bill was organised in Chidambaram, followed by others in Kangayam, Coimbatore and elsewhere, all urging the Madras government to dispense with the Devadasi system. The Isai Vellalar Sangam at Thanjavur and Mayavaram organised meetings in support of the bill.[27] The Telugu Kalavantulus held a meeting in 1927 in Bellary in support of the bill and wrote to Muthulakshmi.

Dr Krishnamurthi writes that their house was always full of musicians and dancers of the Isai vellalar community who used it as a transit place when they came to Madras in search of work or medical attention. There was always food for all of them. And there were pleasant exchanges. If they were upset about the bill, they never showed it. In fact, several delegations came to the house to thank Muthulakshmi.

E. Krishna Iyer, one of the founders of the Madras Music Academy, in a series of letters published in the *Madras Mail*, vehemently protested against Muthulakshmi's attitude towards the Devadasi system and their art known as Sadir. His concern was that the baby, (art), should not be thrown out with the bath water (the system of dedication).

Dance historian, K. Sadasivan writes that the decline of the Devadasi system had actually begun in the 15th century. 'The system declined because of the inherent contradictions presented by what was spiritual and what was temporal. The symptoms of the decline of the system made their explicit appearance during the Nayak period (1565–1800 A.D.) A long tradition of inherent weaknesses and some extraneous factors contributed to the decline. Frequent transfers of Devadasis from temples to other distant places created divisions among them. Except for a few highly influential Devadasis, the majority of them enjoyed very limited liberty and lived on the brink of poverty. They were kept under perpetual watch. There was graded hierarchy.'[28] While the Rudraganikai was permitted to enter the Mahamandapa (main hall) in the temple and perform pure dance (*suddha nritta*) during light worship, the Rudra dasi was permitted only up to the first entrance of the temple. While the Padiyilar (those with no husbands) were granted paddy as remuneration, the Devaradiyars were given some cooked rice balls.[29] The punishments for disobedience were severe from the temple administration and royalty. The decline continued to the 19th Century.

Not satisfied with her first bill, Muthulakshmi, on 24 January 1930 presented a bill to prevent the dedication of women to Hindu temples. The government was concerned that the bill might instigate public disturbances and evoke criticism because it required a stiff penalty of one year's imprisonment for any person taking part in or permitting the dedication of Hindu women to temples.

'There is no doubt that the Devadasi community had some incredibly gifted creative artists with extraordinary skills of music and dance. Aside from the connections to the temples, the practice of women dedicated to the arts privileged the right of wealthy, upper class men to appreciate and enjoy music and dance performances. Not all the practitioners of these arts were great artists, with an instinctive understanding of the muse, and not all their patrons had necessarily any sense of the arts,' wrote the late Keshav Desiraju, former Union Health Secretary.[30]

It has to be recognised that the tradition was deeply flawed. There was no particular status in concubinage and the much vaunted agency of professional courtesans may only have been a way of asserting such independence and dignity as they could salvage out of a fundamentally iniquitous arrangement. That the arts flourished as they did is a tribute to the character and spirit of the women and men who did not have other opportunities.'[31]

Muthulakshmi's language—referring to the Devadasis as victims of the system and promoting the value of continence—was the vocabulary of the moment. 'We all know how sexual promiscuity either in men or women is condemned by all religions and by all good people of any country, and in our country chastity in women has been looked upon as the supreme virtue of womanhood and even supernatural powers have been ascribed to such virtuous women by our poets and philosophers. Under such conditions it surpasses my understanding how sexual promiscuity in a certain class of women has been regarded by the majority of our people as a caste duty and as a thing sanctioned by our religion, and as such tolerated even within the precincts of our holy temples, and again it is beyond my comprehension how in a country which can boast of innumerable saints, sages and rishis, who in their lives have demonstrated to us how much continence in sexual matters contributes to one's physical and mental health and vigour, how irresponsibility in vice has been ignored and even encouraged in men to the detriment of the individual and the future race.'[32]

Historian S. Anandhi says, 'The fear of the upper class Devadasis was that they may be materially downsised because of this legislation. They felt there was no alternate means that was strongly grounded. Muthulakshmi also had the same anxiety and interest that those who were deprived materially needed an alternate avenue. She had met many impoverished women who did not necessarily have land grants and other benefits. They were also worried about their livelihood. Muthulakshmi wanted to give them a wider horizon where they could pursue other careers. So there were two kinds of women who were actually concerned about the livelihood of women.'[33]

The men who opposed the bill were only concerned about culture where women had become the prop to retain traditional culture, dress traditionally and be authentic, while the men themselves could venture into 'modernity'. One must remember that Muthulakshmi was the first woman in the Legislative Assembly and she needed a very strong language to bring out her ideas forcefully before the highly educated upper-class men. She needed a voice of control and authority.

Mahatma Gandhi blessed the bill and supported it through his writings in *Young India*. But when he was arrested in 1930 after his Salt Satyagraha March to Dandi, Muthulakshmi resigned from the Legislative Assembly as a mark of protest. The bill was put aside and became a law only after India gained Independence in 1947. The bill was passed with relative ease because it did not involve any kind of criminal prosecution nor did it require governmental interference in family relationships. By taking away the financial incentive for Devadasis to adopt daughters and dedicate them, the bill set the stage for the gradual abandonment of Devadasi customs, and the subsequent absorption of this unique community into the larger society.[34]

The debate continues to be charged and now, with post-colonial understanding, some generations removed, with a level of critique of modernism, we are able to move into multiple voices, identity politics and victimhood. For this, we must thank pioneers like Dr Muthulakshmi Reddy.

SHELTER OF LOVE

Adi Shakthi, the first woman, who spins the threads of creation, conceives and also destroys in a simultaneity of time, for, in her is alive the wisdom that, in Srishti or creation is the seed of Samhara or destruction....Every ending is a beginning. In Srishti is Samhara, in Samhara is Srishti.

—Pupul Jayakar1

Three young girls knocked on the gates of No 6, Randall's Road, Madras, one day in 1930. Inside the house, Muthulakshmi was rehearsing the speech she would make, to bring about a law to abolish the dedication of young girls as Devadasis. Her sons, Rammohan and Krishnamurthi who were playing in the compound, ran up to the gate. The girls were running away from the ritual of *Bottukattudal*, dedicating them as Devadasis to a deity, and needed protection. Muthulakshmi took them in, and instructed her sons to call them '*Akka*' (elder sister). A few days later she tried admitting them in a hostel. The hostels were all caste-based and would not admit them. Neither would schools. It was then that she decided to house them and educate them herself. Thus was born 'Avvai Illam' (Avvai's Home) for poor and destitute girls.

Since her childhood, Muthulakshmi had been extremely fond of children, and always volunteered to look after babies and infants when their mothers were busy. 'When we see a child, it inspires in us feelings of tenderness and love and even respect for it, for the reason that it is innocent, trustful and helpless, depending on us for protection, food and clothing. In fact, for its very existence, growth and training for the future.'[2]

Soon, seven more girls came to her for shelter, as they were also denied admission in the hostels. Muthulakshmi was disturbed that the women who were coming out of the Devadasi system were abused and labelled by society as morally corrupt. In both her roles as a legislator who appealed to the government to shelter vagrant and destitute children, and as a medical practitioner who spent several hours treating them, Muthulakshmi had an indepth knowledge of the deplorable social conditions these seven girls faced.

She felt an urgent need for a home for children to prevent their exploitation and abuse. There were only two hostels for Hindu girls in Chennai at that time, the Ice House home for young Brahmin widows and one in Triplicane for non-Brahmins. Muthulakshmi was an honorary medical officer for both hostels. However, she felt that what was required was a place where children of all castes can be admitted with opportunities for the improvement of their health, and physical and mental growth.[3] With help from WIA she was able to organise a committee to oversee the setting up of a home for girls.

Mahatma Gandhi led the historic Dandi March against the Salt Law in 1930. When he was arrested, Muthulakshmi resigned from the Madras Presidency Legislative Council in protest. It was that same year that Avvai Home came into existence, registered under the Societies' Act of 1860, with Muthulakshmi as the Honorary Secretary.

A building called Everest on Kutcheri Road in Mylapore was taken on rent for the Home, and Muthulakshmi named it Avvai Home, after the famous ancient Tamil poet Avvai, whom she considered a role model. Avvai Home was the only non-missionary, non-Christian home for girls in Madras Presidency at that time. It started with ten girls, and soon began to receive a steady stream of girls in need of protection and education.

Avvai Home has since trained thousands of women as teachers, midwives, nurses, health visitors, *grama sevikas* (rural social workers) and home makers. The Home has arranged hundreds of marriages for many destitute and homeless girls. There were severe misgivings when Muthulakshmi started the Home, but it still stands today as a home and school where the poorest of girls can access quality education.

Avvai Home was named after Avvaiyar which literally means a *respectable woman*. Avvai was the title of more than one woman poet active during different historic periods in Tamil literature. They were some of the most important women poets of the Tamil canon.

Among them, the first Avvaiyar lived during the Sangam period (3rd century BCE) and is said to have had cordial relations with the Tamil chieftains Vael Paari and Athiyamaan. She wrote 59 poems in *Purananuru*, a collection of 400 heroic poems about kings, wars and public life, of which a few have survived in fragment, into the modern age. She travelled the country, from one village to another, sharing the gruel of the farmers and composing songs for their enjoyment.

The second Avvaiyar lived during the reign of the Chola dynasty in the tenth century. She is often imagined as an old and intelligent woman. Many poems and the *Avvai Kural*, comprising 310 kurals in 31 chapters, belong to this period.

The third Avvaiyar is the old woman most widely known for her *Vinayagar Agaval, Aathichoodi, Kondran Vendhai, Nalvazhi* and *Moodhurai*. These works are didactic in character, and explain the basic wisdom that should govern mundane life. Like Muthulakshmi, Avvaiyar had also found great happiness in the life of young children.

The third Avvaiyar, appealed most to Muthulakshmi, and her statue found a pride of place when Avvai Home moved from Mylapore to Adyar.

Muthulakshmi wanted the children of Avvai Home to be initiated into the language and culture, through Avvaiyar's poems. 'Amma took us all to *Avvaiyar* movie. She had blocked the entire theatre for us children from Avvai Home'[4] says Janaki who was brought to Avvai Home at age six in 1953, and was educated there. She retired as a matron at the Adyar Cancer Institute WIA. Muthulakshmi is supposed to have spoken to close friend S.S. Vasan, producer of the film, and organised a screening for the children. The film *Avvaiyar*, which was among the films celebrating Tamil culture and language, had the story woven around episodes from Avvaiyar's life. The movie had 46 songs which are popular even today.

Avvai Home admitted girls between 4 and 18 years of all castes and creeds. Women above 18 who came seeking admission were sent to other homes for girls, though some were employed at Avvai Home to look after the girls in the orphanage section and the hostel in the mornings and evenings. They were taught reading and writing at other times and a skill for a vocation. No fee was charged for a destitute or a poor girl, but if she had relatives or parents, they were asked to contribute whatever they could towards her maintenance. Muvalur Ramamirthammal, who was working at the grass roots level in the districts to abolish the Devadasi system directed a steady stream of girls to Avvai Home. When the number of girls from Namakkal, Salem and other far-off districts increased, Muthulakshmi needed to find a bigger place.

When World War II began in 1939, several evacuee children from Burma were sent to Madras from Manipur. As no institution was taking children below 10 years then, Muthulakshmi decided to take them all in.

A crisis of sorts occurred when she refused to take girls rescued from brothels into Avvai Home, as her idea for the Home was that of a training institute, and not a correctional facility. This attitude brought in plenty of criticism, and recognition to Avvai Home was cancelled. It was later revealed that these were women sent by her opponents to create trouble at Avvai Home; Muthulakshmi was given advance knowledge about this and hence shrewdly refused them admission[5].

The routine in the Home was strict, and provided an all-round experience of fun and responsibility for all the girls. They had duties in rotation, helping in the kitchen or keeping the campus clean. Janaki, now a retired nurse and matron continuing to work at the Cancer Institute, recalls that they all had to wake up at a certain hour, work in the garden, pick vegetables and complete the duty allotted for the day. An older girl was assigned for a group of every 10 and was responsible for their daily activities and hygiene. She cut their nails, and examined them everyday for dirt, examined their hair for lice and saw to it that they bathed and ate well. It was called a home and not an orphanage and that was the conduct expected of the girls.[6]

In the auspicious month of Marghazhi (15 December—14 January), girls had to wake up at dawn, bathe and sing the Tiruppavai, the verses composed by the female Vaishnavaite Alwar, Andal, at the little temple for the Goddess of learning, Saraswathidevi at Avvai Home. Girls enjoyed drawing colourful kolams (floor patterns) and decorating the whole campus with birds and flowers made with palm leaves.

Only vegetarian food was served in the common dining room. Both Brahmin and non-Brahmin cooks were employed, and women of the Dalit community were among the staff of the Home. By creating a casteless system, Muthulakshmi thought that the girls, when they passed out of the Home, would think about a new social order which did not make caste an important aspect in public life.[7]

The girls had to follow a strict code of conduct at Avvai Home, influenced by the ethical teachings of the *Atichoodi* poem of Avvai, which are as basic as the alphabet. Muthulakshmi wanted the Avvai feel in the age of modern education and employment she was seeking for the girls.

Tamil Letters Uyir Ezhuthu	Athichoodi ஆத்திசூடி	English translation
அ A	அறம் செய விரும்பு Aram seyya virumbu	Intend to do right things
ஆ Aa	ஆறுவத சினம் Aaruvadu chinam	Anger is momentary; do not take decisions during times of anger (in haste)
இ e	இயல்வத கரவேல் Iyalvadu karavael.	Help others based on your capacity
ஈ ee	ஈவத விலக்கேல் Eevadu vilakkael.	Never stop aiding
உ vu	உடையத விளம்பேல் Oolaiyadu vilampael.	Never boast possessions (wealth, skills, or knowledge)
ஊ voo	ஊக்கமத கைவிடேல் Ookkamadu Kaividael.	Never lose hope or motivation
எ ae	எண் எழுத்த இகழேல் Aen elutthu iklael.	Never degrade learning
ஏ aae	ஏற்பத இகழ்ச்சி Aerpadu ikalchi.	Begging is shameful
ஐ ai	ஐயமிட்டு உண் Aimittu unn.	Share what you eat
ஒ o	ஒப்பர வொழுகு Oppura Olagu.	Be virtuous
ஓ Oh	ஓதவத ஒழியேல் Oduvadu Oliyael.	Never stop learning or reading
ஒள Ou	ஒளவியம் பேசேல் Olaviyam Paechel.	Never gossip
ஃ ik	அஃகஞ் சுரக்கேல் Ahkan churukkael.	Never compromise on food grains

Muthulakshmi was responding to the contemporary language of the time when she discussed morals and morality in education in society. For Muthulakshmi, morality and strength went together, and she gave her girls the choice to remain unmarried if they wished to, and pursue a career.

In 1942, during the World War II, soldiers of the British Royal Airforce camping in tents on the banks of Adyar river had made some derogatory remarks about the girls and harassed them. Muthulakshmi stood vigil all night with a stick in her hand and dared any soldier to come near the Home. She even went up the ranks to the commander's house near Fort St. George to complain to him about the conduct of the soldiers, and curb their behaviour.

Sarojini Naidu, hailed as the Nightingale of India, was impressed by the atmosphere at the Home during her visit. In a note to Muthulakshmi, she says, 'I was both moved and delighted by my visit to the Avvai Home orphanage which is one among many beneficial interests of Dr Muthulakshmi Reddy. Her compassionate heart has urged her to provide a shelter of love for girls who are literally the waifs and strays of life. She has abolished all discrimination of class, caste and community. There is an atmosphere of happiness and unity around the children which cannot but influence their minds and character towards sweetness, cleanliness, efficiency and nobility of nature, habit, work and character. It is the personal service and affection given by the founder and her co-workers which makes this so distinctive and delightful.'[8] All the children of Avvai Home received an education. When the Home was in Mylapore, girls were sent to schools nearby, like the Lady Willingdon School or The National School, Sarada Vidyalaya and the Mylapore Convent. Muthulakshmi requested these institutions to give these girls free tuitions and concessions. As a member of the Legislative Council, she piloted a resolution that poor girls studying in any educational institution, government-run, or municipal/government-aided, must be exempted from paying fees up to the Third Form, the equivalent of today's Class 8. The Government which had put this bill into action revoked it in 1934. WIA organised a protest against this with a meeting at the Hindu High School. Muthulakshmi, who was, by now, no longer in the Legislature, wrote several letters to the Government but her pleas fell on deaf ears. Her main rival in the Legislative Assembly, Satyamurthi, now in a position to influence decisions, stalled every one of her bills.

Muthulakshmi decided to start a school in the premises of Avvai Home for its inmates, and children from the surrounding areas. In 1939, a primary school was set up accordingly, which came to be recognised as a special school. She requested the Department of Education to give Avvai Home the liberty of curriculum preparation. Girls were taught household arts, hygiene, childcare, gardening and arts. They learnt *kummi, kolattam* and other dance forms as part of their curriculum.

Avvai Home became the first in Tamil Nadu to start basic education in 1946. Nai Talim or New Education ideated by Mahatma Gandhi with the theme of learning by doing a craft, had a definite programme, with self-sufficiency as the aim at different levels. The children became aware of the dignity of labour, and had to be ready with some skill for a profession. Girls who showed an enthusiasm for studying further were sent to professional colleges, and industrial and vocational schools. Those who had no aptitude for higher studies were imparted skills in spinning, weaving, rattan and mat work, book binding, needlework, dressmaking and housekeeping, along with reading and writing at an industrial centre. The children could earn with their work, at one anna a month in the first grade and about Rs. 1.8 in the fourth grade, making them not only literate but self-reliant too.

Those girls who were deemed too old to begin primary school could still avail of educational experiences. They were all taught languages, maths and writing in the afternoons and evenings by qualified teachers, and trained in some vocational skill.

Muthulakshmi spared no effort in making sure all the girls were suitably placed in life. She used all her powers of persuasion to get people, who were generally judgemental, to accept girls who had risen above their traumatic past. She persevered in finding vocational training programmes or appropriate jobs for them. Depending on their aptitude, they were sent for teacher training or to be trained as midwives, eventually going out of the Home to get jobs as nurses and teachers. In 1936, three women from the adult section of the Home qualified as midwives, and Muthulakshmi found employment for them. Inspired by this, three more women joined the midwives' course that year. Others found placements as part-time cooks and housekeepers in various carefully-vetted households. Many paid their way forward by signing a bond to return the money spent on their training after they began earning, so that others could follow in their footsteps.[9]

In 1935, the WIA office and library were moved to the same building where Avvai Home was located,in Mylapore. The reading room was useful for the girls of the Home. Visitors to WIA, like Sarojini Naidu and Margaret Cousins interacted with the girls and this was certainly an inspiration to them. During the annual session of AIWC, an 'At Home' reception was organised for the delegates, and the girls put up an entertainment programme for the guests.

By then, the number of girls at the Home had increased to 50. There were a large number of applicants, but accommodation facilities were not good enough to increase the number. On her visits to the Theosophical Society, Muthulakshmi saw large tracts of land on either side of Elliot's Beach Road (now called Besant Avenue). Land to the north of the road belonged to the Theosophical Society and to the Thiruvannamalai Sri Arunachaleswara Devasthanams to the south. The land was overgrown with weeds. The temple trustees were not interested in the land but could not sell it under the gift deed. They were, however, willing to lease it out on a long-term basis. Fifty grounds were leased to the Avvai Home at Rs. 10 rental a month, and twenty-seven grounds for Muthulakshmi herself at Rs.18 a month for fifty years, with an option to renew it for another fifty years.

The flow of destitute mothers and children from the districts and villages to Avvai Home did not slow down with the passage of time. The problem became so acute that Avvai Home could not contain all of them. Muthulakshmi successfully submitted a memorandum to the government in 1945 for opening a Women's Welfare Department. Avvai Home correspondingly opened an adult section. They found that the women who came in could look after the children with love and care. Thus adult education also came to be imparted at Avvai Home. The women were put on field work, going from door to door collecting data and monitoring the health and hygiene of people in the locality. Muthulakshmi began a training course in home hygiene, home nursing, craft, dietetics and nutrition, the art of cooking and preservation of food.[10]

In 1932, when Gandhiji was undertaking a fast in Yerawada Jail amid deteriorating health, WIA arranged a prayer meeting in Spur Tank, Egmore. Most of the WIA members were arrested before the meeting.

Muthulakshmi made the necessary arrangements for the management of Avvai Home in case she, too, was arrested, and packed her suitcase. Even with her husband weak and convalescing after a recent illness, she drove to Spur Tank that had been cordoned off by the police. Muthulakshmi broke through the cordon and entered the area marked for prayer, followed by the crowd of students and women. They all sat down, sang prayer songs and hoisted the flag, and ended with the slogan 'Gandhiji ki jai!' Surprisingly, no one was arrested. Muthulakshmi was able to go back to Avvai Home and continue her work.

Avvai Home was a family affair in more ways than one. Initially, Muthulakshmi's sister, C.N. Nallamuthu, was the resident warden of Avvai Home, in addition to a teaching job at Queen Mary's College. In 1934, she married T.V. Ramamurthi whom she had met in England, during her four years at the London School of Economics. Muthulakshmi's son Krishnamurthi describes the events after Ramamurthi visited Nallamuthu. 'He (Ramamurthi) also lived in Mylapore, and soon after his arrival, he visited her (Nallamuthu) on his return from England in 1934. They soon drew the wrath of the intensely conservative Mylapore society of

Edward Elliots Road, and the news reached my mother. My mother was not conservative like Mylapore, she was worse. She was a fanatic puritan, a reaction, probably to environment around her childhood at Pudukkottai. My father had, under mother's influence also lost his English liberal views. My mother raged at the news and sent for her young sister. Mother, was to my knowledge, a very noble and high-minded woman but very dominant and intolerant of what she considered improper. Her attitudes, sometimes, bordered on the tyrannical. My aunt promptly obeyed and came frightened and trembling, yet defiant, reinforced by her quite nervous young man. Mother came straight to the point they had to get married immediately. A registered marriage under the Brahmo Act, as intercaste marriage was still not valid under Hindu law, was suggested. The young man promptly agreed, and his distinguished father promptly disinherited him. Yet they were married as per law in my mother's presence.'

After this marriage, Muthulakshmi and Sundaram Reddy decided to take direct control of Avvai Home. When the Home was shifted to Adyar in 1936, it was Dr Sundaram Reddy who took complete charge of it. He travelled through the districts to collect funds for Avvai Home, which he referred to as Avvai Ashram.

The meagre donations that were coming in were not enough to clothe, feed and educate the girls. So Avvai Home applied for government grants to carry on its work. In 1939, the Home received an annual grant that worked out to less than Rs.1.80 per head per month! Muthulakshmi learnt that missionary orphanages were receiving higher amounts as grants; the civil orphan asylums were given Rs.15 per head per month, and the juvenile delinquents home was given Rs.10 per head per month. This was over and above the administration and infrastructure costs. Muthulakshmi wrote to the Department of Education pointing out the disparities. The home secretary did not see any merit in granting her request to raise the grant.

The couple faced challenges to find funds for the school fees of the girls. Muthulakshmi pleaded for the rule, that girls under the age of five and boys under six years were not eligible for grants, to be changed. The government wrote to her that they were not reopening the subject of fee concessions. While the Reddys were able to find some money for fees, several girls from very poor families had to give up schooling. Even when the then Minister for Education P. Subbarayan pleaded on behalf of the girls, there was no effect. Though Premier C. Rajagopalachari agreed with his minister, he did nothing to change the situation.

In 1952, in partnership with National Centre for Teacher Education and Training, Muthulakshmi started a teacher training institute at Avvai Home offering a two-year diploma course in regional language. Krishnamurthy writes 'The objective was to rapidly generate a teaching cadre to propagate universal education and concomitantly promote professional education and employment.'

In 1964, Nallamuthu, by now retired as the principal of Queen Mary's College, donated a sum for establishing a high school in memory of her husband T.V. Ramamurthi, who had died prematurely, and TVR High School came into being. This school was upgraded to a Higher Secondary School in 1978.

With Muthulakshmi and her son Krishnamurthi getting busy with setting up the Adyar Cancer Institute, her daughter-in-law Mandakini Krishnamurthi took charge as honorary correspondent of the school. Mandakini had spent considerable time at Mahatma Gandhi's Sevagram in Wardha. She developed the curriculum of basic education at Avvai Home, as was needed in the local culture. She was always the first to arrive in school, picking up any trash found on the campus. Girls were always on the alert to pick up trash before she found them. She received many awards for her initiatives in education. Several old students of Avvai Home remember her kindness and untiring work at maintaining cleanliness on the campus, and enthusing girls to study with great fondness. Unfortunately, a debilitating illness prevented her from continuing her work after the year 2000.

In 2001, at the age of 82, Dr Krishnamurthi decided to take responsibility of Avvai Home in addition to his work at the Cancer Institute. Dr Shanta's (a young student of obstetrics and gynaecology, hailing from a well known family of Nobel laureates) sister V. Sushila, just retired from a senior administrative position at the Madras Rubber Factory, came to help. She took over the responsibilities of running the Home as honorary secretary and correspondent, and Rajalakshmi, who had retired as professor of Economics from Ethiraj College, also joined through the good offices of social activist and educator Vasanthi Devi. Very soon, Sugalchand Jain, a distinguished businessman assumed the chairmanship.[11]

By the time it turned 50, Avvai Home had a basic education school, a training centre for teachers, extremely successful skill development programmes and adult education programmes despite the difficulty in finding resources for running the organisation.

Among the innumerable number of women who have benefited by growing up in Avvai Home are Janaki and Punitha. Janaki, who came to Avvai Home as a six-year-old in the late fifties had seen Muthulakshmi 'Amma'. The now 82-year-old, who retired as matron at the Cancer Institute, remembers how loving Muthulakshmi Reddy was, and what a strict disciplinarian she was with the girls.[12]

Punita, who came from an impoverished home, was a bright spark at Avvai Home. She took part in music activities, volunteer services, debates, sports and was a good sportsperson. She is now a school teacher and a young mother. She recalls with gratitude, her days at Avvai Home as the best time of her life.

Krishnamurthi writes, 'Avvai Home was, since its inception, an unplanned project—it was born under an unforeseen emergency. Devadasi reform was expected to herald social changes in that community but the perverse reaction of the so-called social reformers of that time was not anticipated. The Home's development was moulded by a number of factors, environmental changes, political transformations, social evolution and very importantly, the changing needs of society.'[13]

Avvai Home continues to grow amidst a series of difficulties every such organisation faces. The school is situated on the land belonging to the temple. This complicates matters since lack of ownership prevents the Home from applying for building funds for repairs to an 80-year-old building. After Mandakini Krishnamurthi's demise, the house that Muthulakshmi lived in. and the surrounding land was given back to the temple. V. Sushila raised funds to build a sturdy hostel for the girls. She is now getting the building ready for the school with limited seats, on the land donated to the Home by the former chief minister of Tamil Nadu M.G. Ramachandran. Avvai Home continues to flourish, The smiles on the faces of girls at the hostel speak volumes.

C FOR CANCER CARE

The word Cancer evokes varying responses but generally it is one of panic, pain and incurability. To a survivor, it is the memories of the trauma of diagnosis, the various phases in the journey through treatment, follow-up and finally the joy of return to normal living.

—Dr V. Shanta, disciple of Dr Muthulakshmi Reddy[1]

Sundarambal died of cancer in 1923 even as her elder sister Muthulakshmi looked on helplessly, unable to do much for her medically. This death left such an impact on her that she decided to set up a separate hospital for cancer care.

While growing up, Sundarambal was not inclined towards academics as her siblings were. She was given training in music, Sanskrit and Tamil. At 24, Sundarambal joined Queen Mary's College where her younger sister Nallamuthu was teaching. She developed some symptoms of dysentery attributed to the spicy food in the hostel. Muthulakshmi brought her home but the dysentery persisted. Eminent doctors in the city were consulted. One treated her for worms, another gave her emotive injection for amoebic dysentery. In the meantime, Sundarambal received an offer of marriage, that she accepted. The young man was an artist trained in painting at Shanti Niketan, in sculpture in London, and had a job at the School of Fine Arts in Bangalore. The bride was radiant as she left for Bangalore to begin her married life.

Two months later, she wrote to Muthulakshmi that she had conceived, but was suffering from constipation, and had found some drops of blood in the stool. She was treated for constipation in Madras, but when Dr Muthulakshmi examined her, she felt a hard and stony growth on the anterior wall. Shocked, Muthulakshmi suspected malignancy and called Dr Bedon, a well known surgeon at the Women and Children Hospital, Madras. Dr Bedon was also taken aback when she examined her, surprised to see it in a girl looking so healthy. Another doctor saw nothing amiss. Even a pathological examination pronounced the cell normal. But Sundarambal was in extreme pain and a delicate surgery was decided upon, reaching the rectal tumour from behind through the lumbar spine.

As usual, Muthulakshmi took care of all the expenses of treatment.

Muthulakshmi was extremely anxious and brought Sundarambal home to convalesce providing excellent post-surgical care. While dressing the wound, she discovered that a gauze had been left behind in the body; Sundarambal had to endure severe pain as it was cleared and healed. However, the tumour returned.

The treatment of cancer with deep X-Ray and radium was not available in Madras then, and Muthulakshmi sent Sundarambal to Calcutta, and then to Ranchi for radium treatment. Sundarambal's suffering continued, and she passed away in Madras in Muthulakshmi's home.

Muthulakshmi's son Krishnamurthi describes this poignantly. 'The place is a small house on Peters Road, Royapettah, in Madras. The year is 1923 and it is early March. A woman, obviously young but greatly wasted by disease, with lines of pain marked all over her face and hair sparse and wispy, prematurely grey, is lying on a wooden cot. She has passed the stage of despair, and a look of helpless and hopeless misery is in her eyes. She lies quietly on her side, but suddenly writhes and turns when a spasm of pain passes through her shrivelled young body. Another young woman sits in a chair by the cot. She is dark, small made, with a set face. The small chin is determined, and the poise of the little frame bespoke vigour and drive. The most remarkable features, however, are her eyes which glow and sparkle with an innate brilliance. She is dressed in the mode of those times, in a plain kornad saree and a blouse with a high tight fringed collar, and long sleeves reaching up to and fringed at the wrist. The two are sisters, but the suffering of the woman on the bed has wiped out any resemblance between the two. The name of the patient is Sundarambal and the name of the young doctor sister is Muthulakshmi. Sundaram suddenly looks up at her sister and pleads, 'Akka, give me one more shot of morphia please. It does not matter if it is overdose. I would rather go to sleep eternally without knowing it than go through this living death' Her sister turns away her face, set and stern, a world of agony in her eyes, but the mouth and lips stern and firm. 'You have had a grain of morphia just half an hour ago and I am not going to repeat it just now.' Sundaram replies 'But how can you calculate in hours when my pain is not relieved?' Muthulakshmi is silent. She gets up to wipe and clean up the leaking motion and urine through a gaping hole where the anus should have been. Sundaram asks, 'Akka, how long is this to go on? How long am I to be a foulsome burden to you?' Muthulakshmi says 'You are not a burden. This is a service that I would render any patient. So don't be silly.' Sundaram moans 'But Akka, I cannot bear this. I cannot bear this anymore.' That evening Sundaram died. The end came rather suddenly, unexpectedly. The long agony of two years was over for her at last.'[2]

An opportunity to mitigate the agony of women and men suffering from cancer presented itself to Muthulakshmi in 1925, when she went to London where, at the Royal Marsden Hospital, she learnt that the story of cancer need not be only that of despair and failure, that it was possible to cure cancer, and the patient could return to a life of normal activity. She made up her mind to bring home the idea that cancer was no longer incurable. She took an oath to dedicate herself to this cause.[3]

In 1928, back in India and after being nominated as the first woman legislator, among all other causes she was fighting for, Muthulakshmi publicly mooted for the establishment of a separate cancer hospital in Madras. Very few people knew anything about cancer, which they believed spelt most certain death as there was no cure for it. Those who had heard about it attributed it to one's Karma, fate, retribution for one's actions in a previous birth.

Everyone liked Muthulakshmi's idea of a specialty hospital to treat cancer but thought it was not viable. But there was no stopping Muthulakshmi. She possessed a spirit of daring and action, and surged ahead with proposals. In 1935, she moved a resolution at the centenary celebrations of the Madras Medical College for a portion of the funds collected for the celebrations to be earmarked for the establishment of a cancer hospital. No one heeded. In 1936, she presented a memorandum to the King George V Memorial Fund Committee urging that the funds collected should be utilised for a cancer hospital. She requested for a special and separate hospital with modern equipment under specialists to receive patients early and advanced, to give a special course to medical students and post-graduates, and for research work on cancer. She also felt the need for educating the public through the Public Health Department and by volunteer associations, to create an awareness among people about early signs and symptoms of cancer, and on its serious nature when neglected, so that they could get treatment on time.[4]

The appeal had been signed by the president and secretaries of The Madras Presidency Muslim Ladies Association, The Women's Indian Association, Sarada Ladies Union, the Young Women's Christian Association and the Madras branch of All India Women's Conference.

The total lack of empathy and understanding of her plea made Dr Muthulakshmi doubt whether the idea of a cancer hospital would ever be realised in her lifetime. She decided to get her son to believe in her idea and make it happen even if it was after her time. Rammohan, the elder of the two was not interested in Medicine.[5] So, she got her second son Krishnamurthi into medicine in 1937.

Then the World War II in 1939, put on hold all new projects.

Krishnamurthi graduated in medicine in 1942 and was sent to the United States to train in cancer specialty. 'My mother had very little personal wealth,' writes Dr Krishnamurthi in his essay on the initial years of struggle for the Cancer Hospital. 'Father Dr Sundaram Reddy passed away in 1943, and his pension of Rs.500 was suddenly cut off. We had some house property which fetched us a monthly rent of Rs.400, but in the time of rising prices, mother must have been hard put to make both ends meet and yet keep us in the same unaltered comfort as when father was alive. To send me to the U.S. was, however, another matter altogether. Apart from Rs.12,000 cash which father had set aside for my foreign education, mother had no cash capital whatsoever. She sold her car and some other movable property, and with the money launched me in 1947 to the United States of America, in the second phase of her 'Operation Cancer'[6]

After Krishnamurthi's return from the US, Muthulakshmi began fresh efforts for the hospital. He, however, was interested in getting back to the U.S. and had none of the missionary zeal of his mother. 'Nor did I have any inclination to be a heroic pioneer triumphing over odds and ordeals,' he said. His mother sensing his state of mind, changed her tactic completely. Instead of talking to him about service to humanity, she turned on 'emotional blackmail,' explaining in detail all the privations, difficulties and heartbreaks she had suffered in her efforts for the cause of a cancer hospital, how willing she was to face all that suffering only in the hope that her son would one day help her realise her dream. 'I was very attached to my mother. Then and there, we vowed that come what may, we would see the struggle through together,'[7]

Together they approached the Women's India Association (WIA) to conduct a fund-raising campaign for the hospital. WIA was very willing and the Women's Indian Association Cancer Relief Fund was constituted in 1949 with Muthulakshmi Reddy as the treasurer.

The campaign got underway, even though the government turned a cold shoulder to requests for the grant of a land. Muthulakshmi and her son were steadfast in their goal. The Health Minister saw the campaign as a subversion. 'But she was not to be daunted by either Government hostility or public derision. A few of her old friends, however, rallied around her in her moment of trial.'[8]

She decided to hold a public meeting on the question of a proper cancer organisation for Madras State. A sheriff's meeting was called on 18 August 1949 at Rajaji Hall, Madras with prominent figures in public life, doctors, lawyers, businessmen and officials present. The meeting stressed the need for a well-equipped hospital exclusively for cancer, and appealed to the public for funds, and to the Government for cooperation. They collected Rs.1,00,000 in 1952.

'Mother always felt that money collected should, at the earliest date, be converted into building, equipment and work. She was constantly haunted by the visions of past collections by other agencies for other public causes, where the funds could not be traced after some years. She was constantly afraid that if anything were to happen to her suddenly, other forces might come into play which I, being young and unknown, would not be able to combat, and that all her dreams of a Cancer Institute might still come to nothing. She, however, was anxious to obtain land free from Government by alienation, so that the little money available could be used for building and equipment.[9]

Krishnamurthi was then the head of the cancer unit at the Government General Hospital in Madras. This is where Dr V. Shanta, a young student of obstetrics and gynecology met him. Extremely impressed with his quality of fearlessly fighting for ethical medical practice, she changed over to cancer treatment specialty during her house surgeoncy.

In November 1949, Muthulakshmi applied to the State Ministry for Health again for alienation of five acres of land. The reaction was not encouraging. She next approached the minister and secretary for Public Works for the grant of land. Five acres of good land on Mount Road, in the Saidapet region within the city limits,was lying waste and she applied for it. She was told that the land had been reserved for a golf course. She then applied for land in T. Nagar, in Ayodhya Kuppam, and again on Greenways Road, but everywhere the Government had other proposals on hand. She was getting desperate.

In April 1952, the C. Rajagopalachari ministry took over in Madras. There was a proposal to nominate Muthulakshmi to the Legislative Council again but she said she would agree only if land was granted for the cancer institute. The government said a narrow strip of two acres along the eastern banks of the Buckingham Canal, adjoining the new colony of Gandhinagar in the district of Adyar could be made available. The engineers who inspected that land declared it unsuitable for a hospital, but the government bluntly told her 'Take it or leave it.'

Muthulakshmi decided to 'take it'. There was great difficulty in procuring cement and steel to begin work, and she also needed time to collect money to pay the contractors at intervals. In 1953, she applied to the Government of India for a financial grant to meet the expenditure on the building and the equipment. With the help of her friend Durgabai Deshmukh who was then member of the Planning Commission, a grant of

Rs.1,00,000 was sanctioned, and the first block of the Cancer Institute was completed in 1954. In May 1954, the Government of Madras made a grant of Rs.50,000. The first block of the Cancer Institute was formally declared open on 18 June 1954. Muthulakshmi Reddy had realised another dream.

The first block of the Cancer Institute consisted of a small, single storied building, 90 feet by 60 feet, mostly the Sewagram type of huts with thatched roofing. It housed the outpatient department, an office, the radiotherapy and diagnostic rooms, a small dispensary, a small store, a female ward of eight beds,and a male ward of four beds. One of the larger rooms was converted into an operation theatre. The pathology department, where the biopsy studies were done, was housed in an asbestos-enclosed shed.

Most of the surgical equipment were borrowed. Krishnamurthi had brought with him a considerable amount of personal instruments from abroad, including a Zeiss microscope and a Rocker microtome, and these were used in the Institute. The installation of a deep X-ray machine was completed in November. The Institute began to admit patients in January 1955, with all the beds made freely available to the public.

The staff consisted of three honorary medical officers, two paid auxiliary nurses and a paid boy. The nurses were quartered in Muthulakshmi's house in Adyar. Krishnamurti and Shanta had to perform surgeries either very early in the morning or very late in the evening, whenever an anesthetist, working in the other hospitals, was available. Since they could not pay the anesthetist, they adjusted to timings of his availability. Many evenings they began surgery at 8 or 9 pm and finished past midnight. The radiation therapy was carried out in the mornings, and the histopathological work in the afternoons. They did the biopsy, carried the tissues to the pathology shed and put them through the usual processing. The next day they cut the sections themselves, stained and reported them, carried the reports to the wards where they read them again, this time as clinicians.

Food for the patients was cooked at Muthulakshmi's house as there was no kitchen at the Institute and no money to pay the cooks either. It was delivered thrice a day by bicycle.[10]

Dr V. Shanta finished her M.D. in 1954 and had got through the Public Service Commission examination, and was posted to the Women and Children Hospital, a maternity hospital. She would come to the Cancer Institute every day at 2 pm, do the rounds of patients, dress them, give the necessary injections and write the case sheets, complete the daily records in detail and fill up the investigation slips, then clean up the operation theater, pack the sterilizing bins and start the sterilisation. She would personally supervise the sterilisation as there were no trained theatre personnel. She officiated as both a nurse and the surgical assistant during surgeries. She would group and cross match the blood, start the blood transfusion, assist the anesthetist, wash up and lay the table, drape the patient and assist in the operation. All of this was demanding in terms of both time and energy. She had to make a crucial decision. She decided to join the Cancer Institute and moved into the premises, thus making herself available to patients round the clock. The Cancer Institute became her home from 13 April 1955, until her passing on 19 January 2021.

'Amma' (mother), as Shanta called Muthulakshmi, was always around for advice though she was getting frail with age.[11] There were certain fundamentals about which Muthulakshmi was particular, even with a small team and money. One of them was detailed and comprehensive case notes, and another was the biopsying of all tumours and the cytological study of smears. A third was disciplined work, dress code and behaviour which she constantly demanded from everyone associated with her, students or colleagues.[12]

The number of patients at the Institute kept increasing by the day. Patients occupied every inch of available space, and outpatient care was conducted in the corridors. Most patients were poor, and Muthulakshmi made it very clear that they would get the same treatment that a rich patient would. 'This dictum has been both our honour and our burden' said Dr Shanta.[13]

The Institute journeyed through innumerable challenges, trials and tribulations. It took the Institute 10 years to get the Medical Council of India to recognise oncology as a super-speciality. That was not easy. Muthulakshmi, Krishnamurthi and Shanta struggled at every step. When an application was made to the Rockefeller Foundation for funds to buy books for the library, the Directorate of Medical Education of the Tamil Nadu summoned Shanta to explain the need for a library.

In 1955, the Government of Madras gave the institute Rs.5,00,000 in yearly installments of Rs.1,00,00. Jubilant at this, mother and son immediately planned an additional ward of 24 beds. But after work on the building had begun, the government said it was keeping the order in abeyance. Contractors began pressing for their payments. Muthulakshmi and Krishnamurthi went into a huddle. Something had to be done, and quickly. 'Mother took the decision. She said she would risk everything in one final throw, she would appeal to the justice and fair play of K. Kamaraj, the chief minister of Madras. He was known as a very strong man, with a keen insight and an intense sense of justice and a man of firm decisions. Everything depended on the view he took.'[14]

On the morning of 9 September 1956, Muthulakshmi, Krishnamurthi and Dr P. Arunachalam called on Kamaraj, at his residence. He had great regard for Muthulakshmi and ushered her in immediately. On hearing the story, he said in his usual non committal manner, 'Parkalam', 'We shall see.' He called his personal clerk to make a note 'Cancer Institute' in the diary. This was at 9.30 am. At 4.00 pm that day the order releasing the amount reached the Institute by special messenger.

Muthulakshmi was also busy with the Avvai Home and its inmates and curriculum, founding the Avvai Rural Medical Service and the Ramakrishna Vivekananda Free Dispensary for the poor. She opened reading rooms and a library, a Balavadi and crèche to educate small children, was an active member of the Red Cross Society that set up 49 maternity and child care centres in mofussil areas, in addition to serving a second term as Member of the Legislative Council.

Being the pioneer and a first in many areas had become a habit with Dr Muthulakshmi. The Cancer Institute gained the distinction of being the first in the country to install many treatment facilities, though it was an unknown voluntary organisation.

The Institute became a comprehensive cancer centre with a hospital, research centre, division for preventive oncology, and teaching, all through donations. It was declared the first regional cancer centre in 1976.

There are hundreds of happy stories of cancer survivors who are eternally grateful to the Institute,and some sad stories too. One poignant story that Dr Krishnamurthi narrates, in his book *Five decades of Cancer Institute WIA*, is about the time the founder of the DMK and the chief minister of Tamil Nadu, Annadurai was admitted for treatment at the Institute.

'In January 1969, Dr C.S. Sadasivam walked into my out-patient ward with a sheaf of skiagrams of some person unknown. I read them unhesitatingly as advanced recurrent cancer invading the stomach, after an oesophageal resection. I was then told that they were those of the chief minister. The rapidly shifting events of the next two weeks now belong to history, but they were such memorable ones that I shall never forget them. The two legislatures virtually established themselves in the narrow campus of the Institute, and a vast concourse of people gathered in the streets outside. The dividing line was just a few strands of barbed wire. Anna's cabinet colleagues sat quietly and anxiously on benches. MLAs and MLCs strolled in groups in the compound. Yet, for all the mass of VIPs around us, not one hampered or hindered our work. MGR, in his grand manner, as always, provided food for all from his home. They sat on the floor and ate their food and at night they spread their upper cloth on the ground and stretched themselves out, without even a pillow. I could not help but admire the way Anna had trained them, their boundless love and devotion to him, and their implicit submission to his will. The mob outside was, however an entirely different proposition. They were several thousand, strong and composed in the main of the poor. They stood and squatted right along our fence several ranks deep, and overflowed into the lanes and by lanes of Gandhinagar.

They were fairly quiet and orderly at first but as Anna's health deteriorated, the excitement grew and once, a baseless rumour was bruited around and many leapt into our campus. The next few days were critical and the huge mob turned restive. It was then that I grew fearful. The Institute contained much delicate and invaluable equipment, painfully procured over the years by global begging. No grant of rupees could ever replace them and it would have been impossible for us to beg for them all over again. A few minutes of heedless vandalism could destroy years of patient labour. Moreover, there were fifty resident nursing girls and a hundred women patients. Their safety was my charge. The tension was so intense, that on 3 February, I developed cardiac irregularity. But the wisdom of Rajaji and the alertness of Dr M. Karunanidhi saved us from any ugly incident. Rajaji had come to visit Anna and was instantly seized of the potentially explosive situation. He told Dr M. Karunanidhi of his sense of danger, and within a few hours thousands of the armed reserve police had cordoned off the Institute,and none other than those on legitimate business was permitted within a half mile radius. Anna's health was failing hourly. Every one of us was pulling our best, but seemed of so little avail.

Dr Shanta or I were always with him at all hours of the day or night. Even though desperately ill, Anna was always very particular that we should have our food and rest at the proper time, but we could not eat or rest. At near midnight on 3 February one of the greatest of the Tamils passed quietly and peacefully into immortality. We had done our best and failed. Under the circumstances, we could not have done more. I was prepared for the adverse criticism that is the usual penalty for failure. But not for the overwhelming tide of affection and gratitude that the Government and people of Tamil Nadu showered upon us in the weeks that followed. In August of 1969 we had a small function at the Institute. Almost the entire TN cabinet participated. Reviewing the history of our 14 years of tribulation, Dr Shanta asked for 10 acres of land. The Chief Minister, the Hon. Dr Karunanidhi, responded impulsively 'show me the land and I will give it.' A few weeks later we formally submitted our request for land in the Guindy reserve forest, next to Mahatma Gandhi Mantap. There were strenuous objections from the Forest Department and even the Raj Bhavan, but the Chief Minister kept his word, and the land was formally handed over to us in February 1972. Anna had made his bequest!'

This story becomes even more poignant when we remember that Annadurai and Karunanidhi came from the community of Senguntha and Isai Vellalars, and had risen to such high positions with their individual efforts no doubt, but also because of that one woman who founded the Institute, and had also fought in the legislature for the community's shackles to be removed.

Recognition and awards were not slow in coming. Dr Muthulakshmi Reddy received the Padma Bhushan from the Government of India, while Dr Krishnamurthi was awarded the Padmashri. Dr Shanta received the Padma Vibhushan and the prestigious Magsaysay Award, considered Asia's Nobel Prize. Dr Muthulakshmi Reddy was never far from their thoughts, and they frequently credited her with setting out the path for them to follow. 'Our founder's vision' was a phrase they both used in almost every talk about the Institute. The work done by the son and disciple of Dr Muthulakshmi Reddy keeping her vision in mind brought international exposure and appreciation to the Adyar Cancer Institute WIA, which still stands as the most trusted cancer hospital, a living memorial to a far-sighted, committed doctor and social worker Dr Muthulakshmi Reddy.

EPILOGUE

<hr/>

These three, desha, kala and patra, that is,
'the proper place', 'the proper time' and
'the proper person' determine the appropriateness
of an act and thus its meaning.

—Mahabharatha

D r Muthulakshmi Reddy was awarded the Padma Bhushan by the Government of India in 1956. On 30 July 1966, her 80th birthday, a large number of women's organisations in Tamil Nadu honoured her at Rajaji Hall, Madras. On 5 November 1967, she presided over the Golden Jubilee celebrations of Women's Indian Association. 'The strain and emotions of that day proved a little too much for her, and her health began to gradually give way,' writes her son Krishnamurthi.[2]

Through the late 1950s and 60s, she was preoccupied with the welfare of patients at the Cancer Institute, and that of the girls at Avvai Home. Her grandson Sundaram remembers her talking all the time over the phone to someone or the other, to raise funds or get some facilities for these institutions. He read the newspaper to her every morning as her eyesight had begun to fail steadily, due to glaucoma.

Dr V. Shanta fondly remembered Muthulakshmi as being very active in her last years, despite her failing eyesight. "She knew the way around the Cancer Institute so well, that many did not know she could barely see, as she moved around enquiring after the patients."[3]

Muthulakshmi had begun to spend summers in Bangalore to escape the heat of Madras. Rammohan had bought a house there for her, and her faithful help Kanniammal, a refugee from Burma who grew up in Avvai Home, was always at hand. There were also several marriages to be conducted for the girls of Avvai Home. She had arranged a good marriage for her adopted daughter Subbulakshmi, called *Atthai* (father's sister) by Rammohan's and Krishnamurthi's children.

Then there was Narayanasami's brilliant nephew Pitchai, who became the beloved hero of Tamil cinema Gemini Ganesan. He had lost his father when he was just eight years old. Narayanasami entrusted his care to Muthulakshmi before he himself passed on. The boy and his mother were well cared for. She admitted the mischievous boy in Ramakrishna Mission's boys' home. He was fond of his aunt whom he called *Atthai* and made sure his daughters studied medicine, and was himself a big donor to Avvai Home. He inherited the ancestral house of Narayanasami in Pudukkottai, and gave it to Muthulakshmi when she asked him to donate it to a trust to be run as a school for girls. It is now being looked after by Dayanand, a maternal relative of Muthulakshmi as a school for girls. Muthulakshmi had built a home in the Tiruvanmiyur suburb of Madras next to a lake. This house was sold by Krishnamurthi after her passing, and the money donated to Avvai Home. A high-rise has come up on the space now, but a small shrine with her ashes was built in the premises, and is still being tended to by women grateful to Muthulakshmi for their emancipation. The street is now named Dr Muthulakshmi Salai.

Muthulakshmi's family has produced many doctors. Rammohan's son Ramakrishna studied medicine, and had hopes of joining the Cancer Institute but unfortunately passed away in his early twenties. His sister Lakshmi, named Muthulakshmi after her grandmother, and her husband Dr Bhattacharyya are both doctors, and live in retirement in New Delhi.

Dr Krishnamurthi's daughter Chandralekha and her husband are medical practitioners in Australia, while his son Sundaram and his wife are doctors in New York.

Sundaram was studying at the Madras Medical College when his grandmother (whom he called Nanamma) was taken ill in Bangalore and brought to Madras on 18 July 1968. His father told him to visit her as he did not think she would pull through. On 22 July Sundaram went straight to the Cancer Institute from college, and was shocked to find his grandmother's room empty. The lady technician there told him she had been taken home. Intrigued, Sundaram drove home to find a large group of people there, many with sombre faces and some crying loudly. Rammohan and his family had flown down from Delhi. Dr Muthulakshmi Reddy, who had lived every moment of her life achieving impossible dreams, had passed on.

Among the mourners were a large number of people from the Isai Vellalar community. Muthulakshmi's bill to terminate the practice of rendering their service of music and dance in temples had been received with mixed feelings. While some hailed her as their saviour, others opposed her, fearing she was taking away their hereditary art from them. The issue still rages on. While the nostalgists for the Devadasi system bemoan the loss of a culture, many women whose children do not have to suffer the stigma attached to the system send her a quiet prayer of thanks. Muthulakshmi Reddy used the strong language of a liberal, middle-class, educated woman in her arguments, a language which is now being interpreted by some as a voice of control and authority. But such language was needed at that time to claim a level of authority in a legislature that comprised entirely of privileged upper-class men. The people of Pudukkotai mourned a daughter who had made them proud. Even today her achievements resonate in Pudukkotai, with several families naming their daughters Muthulakshmi.

Reams can still be written for and against her work, and debates can continue, but hers was a life lived to the full. She worked with dedication and sincerity with a stubbornly unyielding spirit till she achieved what she felt had to be done.

'Karmany evaa a'dhikaaras tethae
maa phaleshu kathdachana'
(To action alone hast thou a right and
never at all to its fruits)
Bhagavadgita, Chapter II, Verse 47.

ENDNOTES

Breaking Stereotypes

1. Muthulakshmi Reddy, *Autobiography of Dr (Mrs) S. Muthulakshmi Reddy: A Pioneer Woman Legislator* (Madras: M.L.J. Press, 1965), p.5.

2. Private conversation with Dr Sarojini Varadappan, March 2000.

3. Muthulakshmi Reddy, *Autobiography of Dr (Mrs) S. Muthulakshmi Reddy*, p.5.

4. Private conversation with Mr. P. Krishnamurthi, grandson of Narayanasami Iyer's elder brother, Muthusami Iyer, 31 May 2021.

5. Private conversation with Prof. S. Swaminathan. Retired professor IIT Delhi and founder Tamil Heritage Trust Chennai.

6. K.S. Sarwani, *Dr Muthulakshmi Reddy—Social Reformer Par Excellence* (Chennai: Today Publication, 2011) p.17.

7. Private conversation with Dr Uma Jeganmohan, granddaughter of C.N. Ramiah, brother of Muthulakshmi.

8. Private conversation with Mr P. Krishnamurthi, grandson of Narayanasami Iyer's elder brother, Muthusami Iyer, 31 May 2021.

9. Ibid.

10. Muthulakshmi Reddy, *Autobiography of Dr (Mrs) S. Muthulakshmi Reddy*, p.1.

11. Ibid., p.2.

12. Ibid., p.6.

13. Pudukkottai Heritage, a talk by Prof. S. Swaminathan for Tamil Heritage Trust. Video provided by Prof. Swaminathan.

14. Ibid.

15. Ibid.

16. Gopalkrishna Gandhi, ed. *Pudukkottai Tamil Nadu District Gazetteers* (Madras: Government of Tamil Nadu, 1983), p.686.

17. Private conversation with Mr. P. Krishnamurthi, grandson of Narayanasami Iyer's elder brother, Muthusami Iyer, 31 May 2021.

18. S. Santhi, A.R. Saravanakumar. 'Contribution of Dr Muthulakshmi Reddy to Women Empowerment—a Historical Study'. *International Journal of Scientific and Technology Research.* Volume 9, Issue 03, March (2020) p.4.

19. Gopalkrishna Gandhi, ed. *Pudukkottai Tamil Nadu District Gazetteers*, p.693.

20. Muthulakshmi Reddi, *Autobiography of Dr (Mrs) S. Muthulakshmi Reddy*, p.7.

21. Ibid.

22. Ibid. p.9.

23. Ibid. p.17.

24. Gopalkrishna Gandhi, ed. *Pudukkottai Tamil Nadu District*, p.173.

25. Pudukkottai Heritage, a talk by Prof. S. Swaminathan for Pudukkottai - Pudukkottai - Tamil Virtual Academy on 24 January 2014. Recording given to the author by Prof. Swaminathan.

26. Gopalkrishna Gandhi, ed. *Pudukkottai Tamil Nadu District Gazetteers*, p.173.

27. Muthulakshmi Reddi, *Autobiography of Dr (Mrs) S. Muthulakshmi Reddy*, p.12.

28. Gopalkrishna Gandhi, ed. *Pudukkottai Tamil Nadu District Gazetteers*, Preface.

29. Ibid., p.4.

30. K.R. Venkatarama Ayyar, *A Manual of the Pudukkottai State vol II part II.* (Pudukkottai: Sri Brihadamba State Press. 1944), pp.1041–1053.

31. Private conversation with Prof. S. Swaminathan, founder Tamil Heritage Trust, 15.02.2021.

Fox Hill and the Red Building

1. Muthulakshmi Reddy, *Autobiography of Dr (Mrs) S. Muthulakshmi Reddy: A Pioneer Woman Legislator* (Madras: M.L.J. Press, 1965), Introduction.

2. Ibid., p.14.

3. Susan O'Sullivan, 'Women in Medicine: Deeds Not Words,' *The Lancet*, Volume 392, Issue 1015, Sept (2018): 1002–1003.

4. Marilyn Bailey Ogilvie, *Women in Science: Antiquity through the Nineteenth Century, a Biographical Dictionary* (Michigan, United States: MIT Press, 1990).

5. Susan O'Sullivan, 'Women in Medicine: Deeds Not Words'.

6. Ibid.

7. Venkatesh Ramakrishnan, 'Those Were the Days Mary Scharlieb'. *DTNext*, 16 February 2020, (https://www.dtnext.in/News/City/2020/02/16024329/1215477/Those-Were-The-Days-Mary-Scharlieb-the-woman-who-blazed-.vpf).

8. Ibid.

9. *The Indian Express*, 27 September 2010.

10. Muthulakshmi Reddy, *Autobiography of Dr (Mrs) S. Muthulakshmi Reddy*, p.20.

11. Ibid., p.15.

12. Private conversation with Mr. P. Krishnamurthi, grandson of Narayanasami Iyer's elder brother, Muthusami Iyer, 31 May 2021.

13. Ibid.

14. Ibid.

15. Muthulakshmi Reddy, *Autobiography of Dr (Mrs) S. Muthulakshmi Reddy...*

16. S. Muthiah, *Madras Rediscovered* (Madras: East West Publishers, 2006), p.140.

17. Muthulakshmi Reddy, *Autobiography of Dr (Mrs) S. Muthulakshmi Reddy..*

18. *Madras Musings*, Vol.XIX No.4, 1 June 2009.

19. Ibid.

20. Vimala Nayar, *Madras Musings*, Vol.XIX No. 4, 1 June 2009.

21. Website of Madras Medical College, http://www.mmc.ac.in/.

22. Karthik Bhatt, http://madrasramblings.blogspot.com/2009/11/dadha-of-triplicane-mylapore.html .

23. Ibid.

24. Ibid.

Marriage and More...

1. Badrinath Chaturvedi, *The Mahabharata: An Inquiry in the Human Condition* (New Delhi: Orient Longman, 2006) p.358.

2. Muthulakshmi Reddy, *Autobiography of Dr (Mrs) S. Muthulakshmi Reddy: A Pioneer Woman Legislator* (Madras: M.L.J. Press, 1965), p.19.

3. Ibid.

4. Nandini Chatterjee, published online by Cambridge University Press 18 June 2010. https://ore.exeter.ac.uk/repository/bitstream/handle/10871/14924/Chatterjee_CSSH_2010.pdf?sequence=2&isAllowed=y

5. V.R. Anil Kumar, *Vivaha Samskara in Grihya Sutras of the Four Vedas.* (New Delhi D.K. Printworld, 2014) p.297.

6. Muthulakshmi Reddy, *Autobiography of Dr (Mrs) S. Muthulakshmi Reddy*, p.19.

7. Ibid., p. 20

8. Ibid., p.21.

9. Ibid., p 21.

10. Private conversation with P. Krishnamurthy, a nephew of Narayanasami, as told to him by his grandmother Lakshmi, a close confidante of Chandrammal.

11. Ibid.

12. Muthulakshmi Reddy, *Autobiography of Dr (Mrs) S. Muthulakshmi Reddy*, p.24.

13. Ibid., p.24.

14. Ibid., p.28.

15. K.S. Sarvani, *Dr Muthulakshmi Reddy—Social Reformer Par Excellence* (Chennai: Today Publication, 2011) p.22.

Theatre of Life

1. Muthulakshmi Reddy, *Autobiography of Dr (Mrs) S. Muthulakshmi Reddy: A Pioneer Woman Legislator* (Madras: M.L.J. Press, 1965) p.133.

2. https://sriramv.wordpress.com/2012/08/03/from-widows-hometo-vivekanandar-illam/

3. Monica Felton, *A Child Widow's Story* (New Delhi: Katha Publications, 2004).

4. K.S. Sarvani, *Dr Muthulakshmi Reddy—Social Reformer Par Excellence* (Chennai: Today Publication, 2011) p.21.

5. Sarah K. Broome. 'Stri-Dharma: Voice of the Indian Women's Rights Movement 1928–1936.' Thesis, Georgia State University, 2012.

6. Ibid.

7. Vineet Krishna, clpr.org.in/blog/the-womens-indian-association and-india-constitutional-thought-part.

8. Geraldin H. Forbes, *Women in Modern India* (Cambridge, England: Cambridge University Press, 1998) pp71–82.

9. Ibid., pp.85, 89.

10. Sarah K. Broome. 'Stri-Dharma: Voice of the Indian Women's Rights Movement 1928–1936.'

11. Private conversation with Ram Suryanarayan, a relative of Dr Muthulakshmi Reddy, 20 June 2021.

12. Muthulakshmi Reddy, *Autobiography of Dr (Mrs) S. Muthulakshmi Reddy,* p.35.

13. Conversation with Subbulakshmi's grandson Ram Suryanarayan, 20 June 2021.

14. Ibid.

15. Ibid.

16. Ibid

17. Muthulakshmi Reddy, *Autobiography of Dr (Mrs) S. Muthulakshmi Reddy*, p.42.

18. Muthulakshmi Reddy, *Autobiography of Dr (Mrs) S. Muthulakshmi Reddy*, p.104. (She went to England to give evidence for women's issues in the meetings that took place along with the third Round Table Conference).

19. Now Sri Lanka.

[There is no note indicator 19 in the chapter. Place 19 on p.99 line 1 after the word 'precision.']

Yugadharma and Creative Citizenship

1. Bhikhu Parekh, *Colonialism, Tradition and Reform: An Analysis of Gandhi's Political Discourse* (New Delhi: Sage Publications, 1989). p.19.

2. *Muthulakshmi Reddi, Autobiography of Dr (Mrs) S. Muthulakshmi Reddy: A Pioneer Woman Legislator* (Madras: M.L.J. Press, 1965), p.51.

3. Interview with Sarojini Varadappan, a close confidante of Dr Muthulakshmi Reddy, 23 July 1994.

4. Bhikhu Parekh, *Colonialism, Tradition and Reform*, p.20.

5. *Muthulakshmi Reddy, Autobiography of Dr (Mrs) S. Muthulakshmi Reddy*, p.51.

6. K.S. Sarvani, *Dr Muthulakshmi Reddy—Social Reformer Par Excellence* (Chennai: Today Publication, 2011), p.49.

7. *Muthulakshmi Reddy, Autobiography of Dr (Mrs) S. Muthulakshmi Reddy*, p.171.

8. From the brochure of the AIWC.

9. Geraldine Forbes, 'Caged Tigers: "First Wave" Feminists in India,' *Womens Studies International Forum*, State University of New York at Oswego (December 1982): 525–535.

10. Ibid.

11. Ibid.

12. V. Venktaraman, 'Simon Go Back! Reflections of the Indian Press on the Boycott of Simon Commission in the Madras Presidency, 1928–1930', *SSRN Electronic journal* (August 2019).

13. *Muthulakshmi Reddy, Autobiography of Dr (Mrs) S. Muthulakshmi Reddy*, p.58.

14. http://www.kkhsou.in/main/education/hartog_committee

15. Ibid.

16. Ibid.

17. K.S. Sarvani, *Dr Muthulakshmi Reddy—Social Reformer Par Excellence*, p.49.

18. *Muthulakshmi Reddy, Autobiography of Dr (Mrs) S. Muthulakshmi Reddy*, p.23

19. Ibid., p.54.

20. Dr S. Krishnamurthy, *Five decades of the Cancer Institute WIA*. (Chennai: Cancer Institute WIA on the occasion of its golden jubilee 2004), p.5.

The Devadasi Question

1. Muthulakshmi Reddy, 'Anti Nautch Movement', *Madras Mail*, 17 December 1932.

2. Ibid.

3. Saimata Sivabrindadevi in a letter to editor. *Sruti Magazine*, 149, February (1997): 5, 6.

4. Dr S. Krishnamurthy. Interview to the author on 3 August 1998.

5. K. Sadasivan, *Devadasi System in Medieval Tamil Nadu* (Chennai: Akani Veliyeedu 2011), p.53.

6. Interview with P. Krishnamurthy, grandnephew of Narayasami Iyer, narrated to him by his grandmother.

7. Ibid.

8. Ibid.

9. Muthulakshmi Reddy *Autobiography of Dr (Mrs) S. Muthulakshmi Reddy: A Pioneer Woman Legislator* (Madras: M.L.J. Press, 1965), p.16.

10. Conversation with Dr Uma Jeganmohan, grandniece of Dr Muthulakshmi Reddy.

11. B. Jeevasundari. *Muvalur Ramamirtham Vazhkai Panium* (Tamil) (Bharati Puthakalayam, 2017) p.37.

12. Ibid, p.39.

13. K. Sadasivan, *Devadasi System in Medieval Tamil Nadu* (Chennai: Akani Veliyeedu 2011).

14. Conversation with Booma Srinivasan at the WIA office in Chennai, 14 March 2021.

15. Ibid.

16. B. Jeevasundari. *Muvalur Ramamirtham Vazhkai Panium* (Tamil) (Chennai: Bharati Puthakalayam,2017), p.44.

17. Information provided by the granddaughter of Muvalur Ramamirtham to P. Jeevasundari passed on to the author.

18. Phone conversation with Vaasanthi on 6 September 2021.

19. T.G.P. Spear, *The Nabobs* (London: Oxford University Press, 1932), p.34.

20. B. Jeevasundari. *Muvalur Ramamirtham Vazhkai Panium* (Tamil) (Chennai: Bharati Puthakalayam,2017), p.168.

21. Ibid., p 169

22. Conversation with B.Jeevasundari on 23 June 2021

23. Dr S. Krishnamurthi. *Mother and Avvai Home.* Handwritten personal papers collected at Avvai Home.

24. Dr Muthulakshmi Reddy, Article in *Revolt,* 17 November 1929, compiled in *Revolt—A Radical Weekly in Colonial Madras,* edited by V. Geetha and S.V. Rajadurai (Periyar Dravida Iyakkam 2008), p.411.

25. Ibid.

26. Ibid.

27. B. Jeevasundari. *Muvalur Ramamirtham Vazhkai Panium* (Tamil) (Chennai: Bharati Puthakalayam,2017), p.118.

28. *Annual Report on Indian Epigraphy* 1918–1921. No.230 https://www.tamildigitallibrary.in/

29. R. Nagaswamy, 'Devadasi of Tamil Nadu'. Article in the *Sangeet Natak* magazine issue July–September 1990

30. Keshav Desiraju, *Of Gifted Voice: The Life and Art of M.S. Subbulakshmi* (New Delhi: Harper Collins, 2021), p.23.

31. Ibid., p.25.

32. Ibid., pp.147, 148.

33. S. Anandhi, talk on telephone on 19 December 2020.

34. Kay K. Jordan. *From Sacred Servant to Profane Prostitute* (New Delhi: Manohar Publishers, 2003), p.134.

Shelter of Love

1. Pupul Jayakar, *The Earth Mother* (New Delhi: Penguin Books, 1989), Preface.

2. Muthulakshmi Reddy, typewritten speech perused at Avvai Home. Perused on 17 June 2021

3. Ibid.

4. Recorded oral interview with Janaki at the Cancer Institute on 28 June 2021.

5. Recorded oral interview with Narayanaswami's grand-nephew P. Krishnamurthi.

6. Recorded oral interview with Janaki at the Cancer Institute on 28 June 2021.

7. K.S. Sarvani, *Dr Muthulakshmi Reddy—Social Reformer Par Excellence* (Chennai: Today Publication, 2011), p.137.

8. Published in Avvai Home silver jubilee souvenir 1955. Perused on 17 June 2021.

9. K.S. Sarvani, *Dr Muthulakshmi Reddy—Social Reformer Par Excellence*, p.139.

10. Ibid.

11. *My Mother and Avvai Home*. Notes written by Dr S. Krishnamurthy perused at Avvai Home.

12. Recorded oral interview with Janaki at the Cancer Institute on 28 June 2021.

13. *My Mother and Avvai Home*. Notes written by Dr S. Krishnamurthy collected at Avvai Home on 17 June 2021.

C for Cancer Care

1. Dr V. Shanta, *My Journey Memories: Cancer Institute WIA*. (Chennai: 2013), Acknowledgments.

2. Dr S. Krishnamurthy, *Five decades of the Cancer Institute WIA*. (Chennai: Cancer Institute WIA on the occasion of its golden jubilee, 2004), p. 15,16.

3. Ibid., p.3.

4. Ibid., p.5.

5. Conversation with Dr Lakshmi Bhattacharya, daughter of Rammohan on 15 May 2021.

6. Dr S. Krishnamurthi. *Five decades of the Cancer Institute (WIA): 1954—2004*, p.22.

7. Ibid. p. 22.

8. Personal Interview with Dr.Krishnamurthy held on 23 August 1998.

9. Dr S. Krishnamurthi. *Five decades of the Cancer Institute (WIA): 1954—2004*, p.26.

10. An informal interview with Dr V. Shanta on 19 August 2011.

11. Ibid.

12. Ibid.

13. Ibid.

14. Dr S. Krishnamurthy, *Five decades of the Cancer Institute WIA*, p.35.

Epilogue

1. Chathurvedi Badrinath, *The Mahabharatha: an Enquiry into the Human Condition* (New Delhi: Orient Longman, 2007), p.9.

2. Dr S. Krishnamurthy, *Five decades of the Cancer Institute WIA. Chennai*, (Chennai: Published by the Cancer Institute WIA on the occasion of its golden jubilee, 2004), p.6.

3. Informal interview with Dr V. Shanta on 3 December 2019.

OTHER PUBLISHED BOOKS
in this new series